GRADE

MW00574146

everyday

Vocabulary

Intervention Activities

Table of Contents

Using Everyday Vocabulary Intervention Activities

Current research identifies vocabulary and word study as essential skills for reading success. Before children learn to read, they need to be aware of the meaning of words. Vocabulary instruction teaches children how to determine the meanings of words by utilizing contextual and conceptual clues. Word-study and word-solving strategies help children build their vocabularies, which leads to increased reading comprehension.

Effective vocabulary activities provide students with opportunities to:

- Actively engage in learning more about words and how words work
- Build their vocabularies and gain greater control of language
- Develop the ability to use context clues to define unfamiliar words
- Develop and build content vocabulary

Although some students master these skills easily during regular classroom instruction, many others need additional reteaching opportunities to master these essential skills. The Everyday Vocabulary Intervention Activities series provides easy-to-use, five-day intervention units for Grades K–5. These units are structured around a research-based model-guide-practice-apply approach. You can use these activities in a variety of intervention models, including Response to Intervention (RTI).

Getting Started

In just five simple steps, Everyday Vocabulary Intervention Activities provides everything you need to identify students' needs and to provide targeted intervention.

online

1. PRE-ASSESS to identify students' vocabulary needs.

Use the pre-assessment to identify the skills your students need to master.

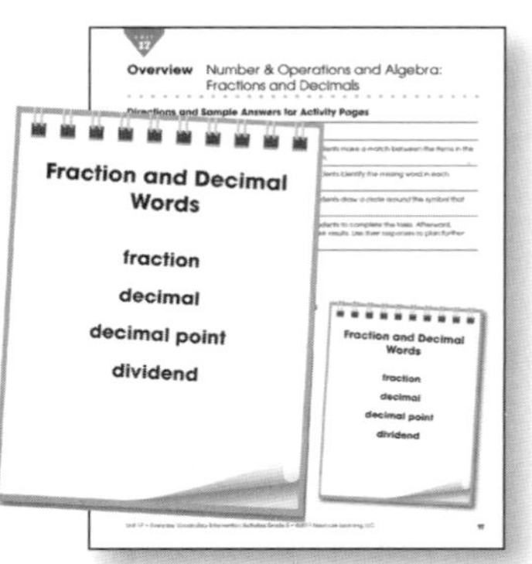

Day 1

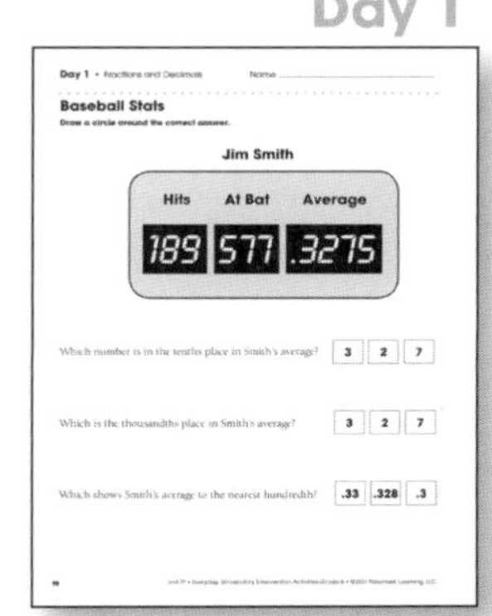

2. MODEL the skill.

Every five-day unit targets a specific vocabulary or word study strategy. On Day 1, use the teacher prompts and reproducible activity page to introduce and model the skill.

Day 2 Day 3 Day 4

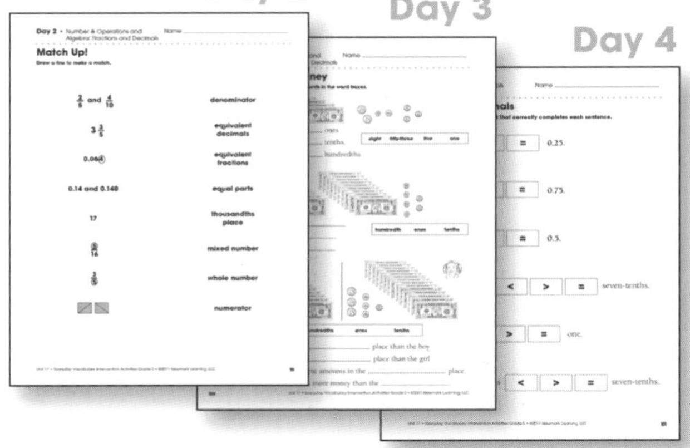

3. GUIDE, PRACTICE, and APPLY.

Use the reproducible practice activities for Days 2, 3, and 4 to build students' understanding and skill proficiency.

Day 5

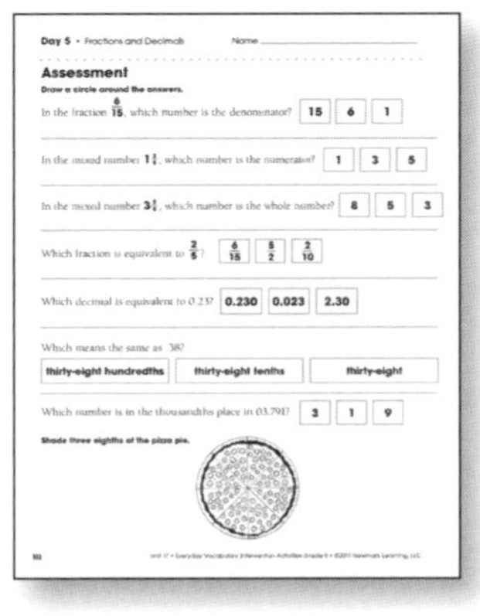

4. MONITOR progress.

Administer the Day 5 reproducible assessment to monitor each student's progress and to make instructional decisions.

5. POST-ASSESS to document student progress.

Use the post-assessment to measure students' progress as a result of your interventions.

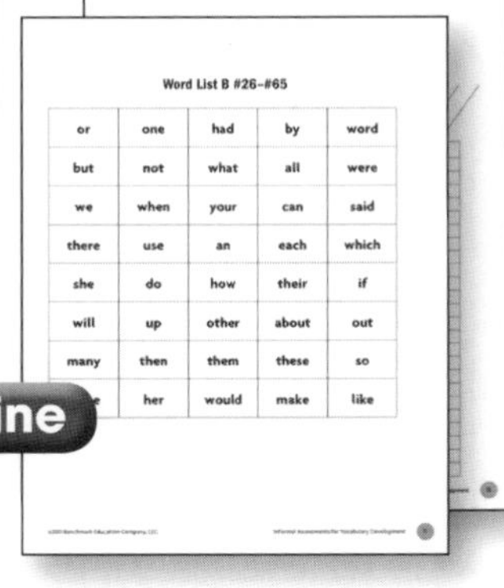

online

Standards-Based Phonemic Awareness Skills in Everyday Intervention Activities

The vocabulary words and strategies found in the Everyday Intervention Activities series are introduced developmentally and spiral from one grade to the next. The chart below shows the types of words and skill areas addressed at each grade level in this series.

Everyday Vocabulary Intervention Activities Series Skills	K	1	2	3	4	5
Sight Words	✔	✔	✔	✔		
Nouns, Pronouns, and Proper Nouns	✔	✔	✔	✔	✔	✔
Verbs	✔	✔	✔	✔	✔	✔
Adjectives	✔	✔	✔	✔	✔	✔
Synonyms and Antonyms	✔	✔	✔	✔	✔	✔
Compound Words		✔	✔	✔	✔	✔
Multiple-Meaning Words	✔	✔	✔	✔	✔	✔
Classify Words by Subject	✔	✔	✔	✔	✔	✔
Word Analogies	✔	✔	✔	✔	✔	✔
Word Parts and Root Words	✔	✔	✔	✔	✔	✔
Word Webs and Diagrams	✔	✔	✔	✔	✔	✔
Using Words in Context	✔	✔	✔	✔	✔	✔
Using Context Clues to Determine Word Meaning				✔	✔	✔
English/Language Arts Content Words	✔	✔	✔	✔	✔	✔
Social Studies Content Words	✔	✔	✔	✔	✔	✔
Science Content Words	✔	✔	✔	✔	✔	✔
Math Content Words	✔	✔	✔	✔	✔	✔

Using Everyday Intervention for RTI

According to the National Center on Response to Intervention, RTI "integrates assessment and intervention within a multi-level prevention system to maximize student achievement and to reduce behavior problems." This model of instruction and assessment allows schools to identify at-risk students, monitor their progress, provide research-proven interventions, and "adjust the intensity and nature of those interventions depending on a student's responsiveness."

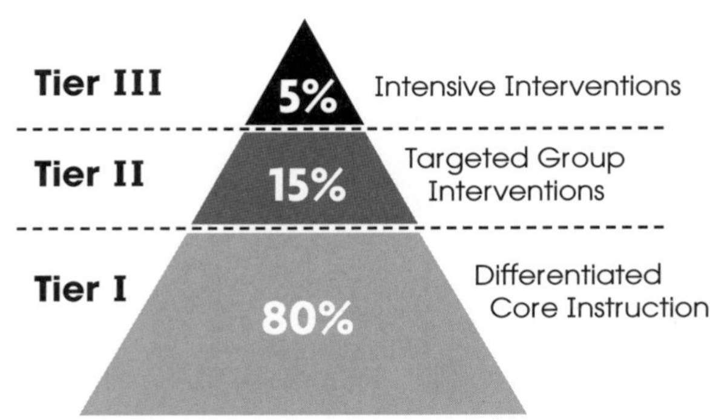

RTI models vary from district to district, but the most prevalent model is a three-tiered approach to instruction and assessment.

The Three Tiers of RTI	Using Everyday Intervention Activities
Tier I: Differentiated Core Instruction • Designed for all students • Preventive, proactive, standards-aligned instruction • Whole- and small-group differentiated instruction • Ninety-minute, daily core reading instruction in the five essential skill areas: phonics, phonemic awareness, comprehension, vocabulary, fluency	• Use whole-group vocabulary mini-lessons to introduce and guide practice with vocabulary strategies that all students need to learn. • Use any or all of the units in the order that supports your core instructional program.
Tier II: Targeted Group Interventions • For at-risk students • Provide thirty minutes of daily instruction beyond the ninety-minute Tier I core reading instruction • Instruction is conducted in small groups of three to five students with similar needs	• Select units based on your students' areas of need (the pre-assessment can help you identify these). • Use the units as week-long, small-group mini-lessons.
Tier III: Intensive Interventions • For high-risk students experiencing considerable difficulty in reading • Provide up to sixty minutes of additional intensive intervention each day in addition to the ninety-minute Tier I core reading instruction • More intense and explicit instruction • Instruction conducted individually or with smaller groups of one to three students with similar needs	• Select units based on your students' areas of need. • Use the units as one component of an intensive vocabulary intervention program.

Overview Nouns, Pronouns, Possessives, and Proper Nouns

Directions and Sample Answers for Activity Pages

Day 1	See "Provide a Real-World Example" below.
Day 2	Read aloud the title and directions. Help students cut out the words and identify each as a pronoun, possessive, or proper noun. Then guide them to glue each word in the correct column.
Day 3	Read aloud the title and directions. Divide the class into small groups. Help them cut out one set of words, fold them, and put them in a container. Guide students to take turns picking a word, stating if they are a person, place, or thing, and then acting out who or what they are.
Day 4	Read aloud the title and directions. Help students read the sentences and find the missing word in the word box. Model how to write the word into the crossword puzzle.
Day 5	Read aloud the directions. Allow time for students to complete the task. Afterward, meet individually with students to discuss their results. Use their responses to plan further instruction and review.

Provide a Real-World Example

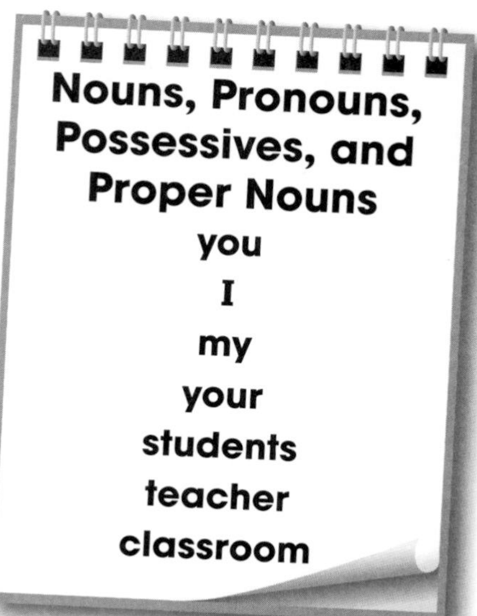

- **Say:** *You are my students. I am your teacher! This is your classroom.* As you say the sentences, write them on chart paper or the board. Point to the words **you** and **I**. Remind students that these are pronouns, or words used in place of a noun. Write **you** and **I** on chart paper. Ask students to share other pronouns they know. Add their ideas to the chart paper.
- Point to the words **my** and **your** in the sentences. Remind students that these words are possessive pronouns, or pronouns that show ownership. Write **my** and **your** on the chart paper.
- **Say:** *A regular, or common, noun names a person, place, or thing. Which words in these sentences name people? Which names a place?* (Allow responses.) Then write **students**, **teacher**, and **classroom** on the chart paper. Point out that **teacher** and **classroom** are singular because there is only one of each. **Say:** *We add an **s** to **student** because there is more than one student. There are lots of you. When there is more than one noun, we say it's a plural noun.*
- **Ask:** *What's the name of our school?* Write their response on the chart paper. Then **ask:** *What is your name? What is my name? What is the principal's name?* Write their responses on the chart paper. Then **say:** *The names of specific people, places, and things are proper nouns. Proper nouns begin with an uppercase letter. What are some other proper nouns you know?* Write their ideas on the chart paper.
- Hand out the Day 1 activity page. Read aloud the directions. **Say:** *The pronoun **you** is the only word that makes sense in this question. I see **you** in the word box. I will write it on the line.* Draw attention to the next sentence. Point out that the missing word is the reflexive pronoun **myself**. Continue to help students as needed.

Cloze It Up!

Read the sentences. Use the words in the word box to complete each sentence. Write the words on the lines.

dictionary	her	library	myself	Officer Jones
our	planets	railroad station	they	you

Where are ____________ going?

I can do it ____________!

____________ name is Maya.

____________ keeps our town safe.

We use a ____________ when we don't know what a word means.

Carlos borrows books from the ____________ every week.

My parents take the train to work. ____________ go to the ____________ to catch the train.

There are eight ____________ in the solar system. Earth is ____________ planet.

 Name ______________________

The Three Ps

Cut out the words. Identify each as a possessive, a proper noun, or a pronoun. Glue the words in the correct columns.

Possessive	Proper Noun	Pronoun

Elm Road	her	Holly	it	its
my	Jones Beach	ours	Ryan	she
their	us	we	he	they

Act It Out!

Cut out the words, fold them, and put them in a container. Take turns acting out the nouns for the class to guess. Provide a hint by stating whether you are a person, place, or thing.

grandfather	**doctor**	**firefighter**	**sister**
calendar	**computer**	**beach**	**playground**
flower	**whale**	**sun**	**robot**
sheep	**zoo**	**phone book**	

Crossword Puzzle

Read the clues. Find the missing words in the word box. Write the words in the crossword puzzle.

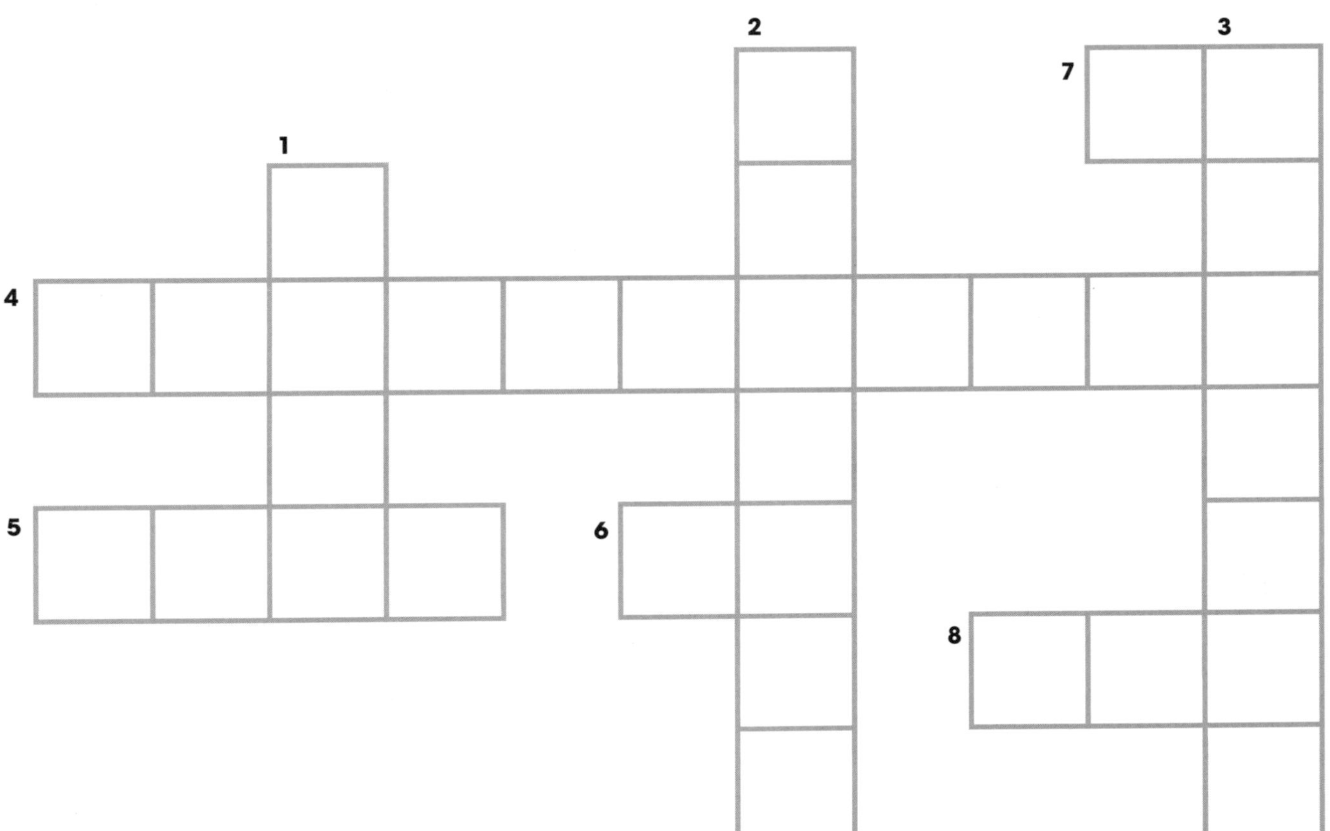

herself
mine
moon
our
photographs
sisters
us
we

Clues

Down

1. The ____________ moves around Earth.
2. The girl walks by ____________ to school.
3. Jenny and Maria are my older ____________.

Across

4. I take ____________ with my camera.
5. The puppy is ____________.
6. ____________ live in a red house.
7. We took them with ____________.
8. They are ____________ friends.

Assessment

Read the passage. Circle the word or words that complete the sentence. Write the word on the line.

When the United States was new, ____________________ wanted
Americans **Africans**

____________________ country to have ____________________ own flag.
their **your** **his** **its**

The first ____________________ was made in 1777. ____________________
flag **American** **It's** **It**

had seven red stripes and six white ____________________.
symbols **stars**

When people think of the United States, ____________________ often think
they **us**

of the bald ____________________. When the United States was a new
our **eagle**

country, ____________________ leaders wanted to choose a national bird.
his **its**

One leader, ____________________, wanted the
White House **Benjamin Franklin**

national bird to be the wild turkey. Other leaders thought the bald eagle was

a more powerful ____________________. The bald eagle became the official
bird **bear**

national bird of the ____________________ in 1782.
United States **New York City**

If ____________________ look closely at a dollar bill, you will see the Great
you **she**

Seal of the United States. ____________________ leaders created this
Their **Our**

seal on July 4, 1776. ____________________ wanted a symbol to represent the
They **You**

new nation.

Overview Action Verbs

Directions and Sample Answers for Activity Pages

Day 1	See "Provide a Real-World Example" below.
Day 2	Read aloud the title and directions. Help students read the clues and find the verbs in the word box. Model how to write a word into the crossword puzzle.
Day 3	Read aloud the title and directions. Divide the class into small groups. Help them cut out one set of words, fold them, and put them in a container. Tell students they can speak while acting out the word, but they can't say the verb.
Day 4	Read aloud the title and directions. Help students read the sentence and write the verb that completes it on the line.
Day 5	Read aloud the directions. Allow time for students to complete the task. Afterward, meet individually with students to discuss their results. Use their responses to plan further instruction and review.

Provide a Real-World Example

- Do jumping jacks or jog in place as you **say:** *I am exercising.* ***Exercise*** *is a verb.* Write **exercise** on chart paper or the board. Remind students that a verb is a word that describes what a person or thing is doing, thinking, or feeling. Point out that exercising is something we do. Now stop exercising and **say:** *I exercised.* Write **exercised** on the chart paper. Point to the suffix **-ed** and **say:** *When we describe something we did in the past, we usually add the letters* ***-ed*** *to the end of the verb.*

- Now look at a picture on the classroom wall and smile. **Say:** *I am admiring the picture.* ***Admire*** *is a verb that means to look at and enjoy.* ***Admire*** *is a verb that describes what a person is thinking.* Write **admire** on the chart paper. Now **say:** *I adore chocolate. It is my very favorite food!* Explain that **adore** is a verb that means to really love something. **Adore** describes what a person feels. Write **adore** on the chart paper.

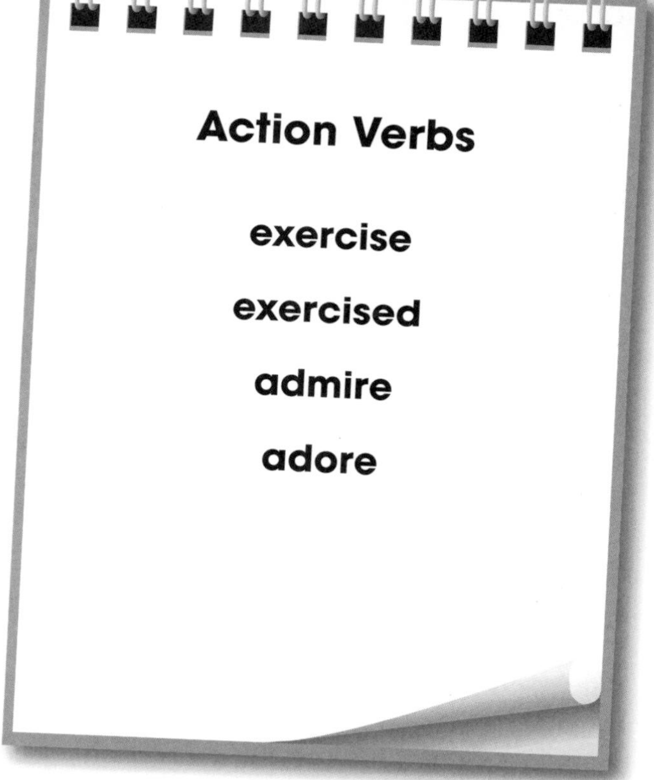

- Hand out the Day 1 activity page. **Say:** *Let's look at some verbs and decide if each one is a doing, thinking, or feeling verb.* Draw students' attention to the first word, **believe**. **Say:** *You can't see someone believe something.* ***Believe*** *is a verb that describes what someone is thinking. Let's write* ***believe*** *in the "Thinking" column.* Read aloud the next verb, **bellow**. **Say:** *When you bellow, you shout. Shouting is something we do. Let's write the word* ***bellow*** *in the "Doing" column.* Continue guiding students as needed.

Name ______________________________

Doing, Thinking, Feeling

Write doing verbs under the jogger. Write thinking verbs under the lightbulb. Write feeling verbs under the heart.

believe	**bellow**	**bore**	**compare**	**comprehend**	**concentrate**
determine	**disappoint**	**examine**	**introduce**	**memorize**	**remember**

Doing 	**Thinking**	**Feeling**

 Name ____________________

Crossword Puzzle

Read the clues. Find the verbs in the word box. Write the verbs in the crossword puzzle.

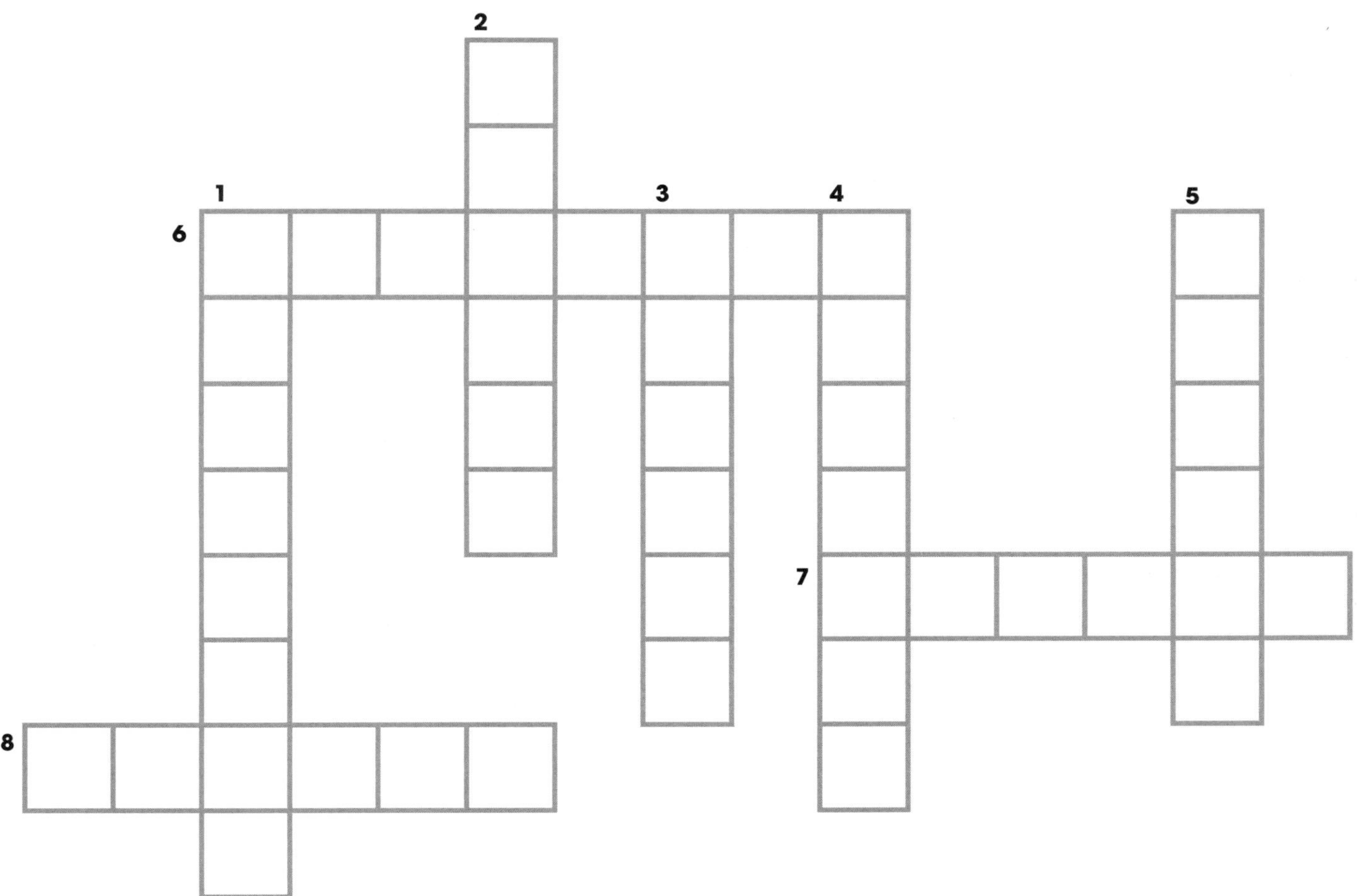

absorb
advise
badger
compress
converse
dampen
exhibit
recall

Clues

Down

1. to press or squeeze something to fit into a small space
2. to give suggestions
3. to remember something
4. to show something to the public
5. to make something moist or wet

Across

6. to talk with someone
7. to keep asking someone to do something
8. to soak up

Name ______________________________

Act It Out!

Cut out the words, fold them, and put them in a container. Take turns acting out the verbs for classmates to guess. Use the word box for clues.

admit	babble	bathe	befriend	bore
copy	disappear	examine	pester	recite

admit	babble	bathe	befriend	bore
copy	disappear	examine	pester	recite

 Name ________________

Finish the Sentence

Read each sentence. Write the word that best completes it on the line.

The burglar finally ________________ to the crime.

confessed **conversed**

Don't ________________ your sister while she is studying!

blockade **bother**

If you practice, you will ________________.

claim **succeed**

Charlie is polite. He always ________________ to say "please" and "thank you."

remembers **replaces**

Blood ________________ through your body.

circulates **summarizes**

When the principal yells, the children ________________.

cower **claim**

In a war, one side ________________ the other.

adapts **attacks**

The candidate tried to ________________ us to vote for him.

proclaim **persuade**

The puppy ________________ his new surroundings.

explained **explored**

The mall ________________ many people from the community.

employs **enforces**

Name ______________________________

Assessment

Draw a line to match verbs that have the same meaning.

adapt	**understand**
babble	**convince**
bother	**hire**
comprehend	**change**
employ	**recall**
exhibit	**pester**
persuade	**talk excitedly**
remember	**show**

Overview Describing Words

Directions and Sample Answers for Activity Pages

Day 1	See "Provide a Real-World Example" below.
Day 2	Read aloud the title and directions. Help students read each sentence and identify the adjective or adverb. Then help them find the words in the word find. (**Adjectives:** absorbent, irresponsible, optimistic, irritating; **Adverbs:** gracefully, gravely, generously, cautiously)
Day 3	Read aloud the title and directions. Help students identify the word that correctly completes the sentence and write it on the line.
Day 4	Read aloud the title and directions. Help students read the clues and find answers in the word box. Model how to write a word into the crossword puzzle.
Day 5	Read aloud the directions. Allow time for students to complete the task. Afterward, meet individually with students to discuss their results. Use their responses to plan further instruction and review.

Provide a Real-World Example

- **Ask:** *If an ice cream seller gives generous scoops of ice cream, is that a lot or a little ice cream?* Write **generous** on chart paper or the board. (Allow responses.) Then **say:** ***Generous*** *means "a lot."* ***Generous*** *is an adjective, a word that describes a noun. In this case,* ***generous*** *describes the amount of ice cream.*

- **Ask:** *If you give generously to a charity, does it mean you give a lot or a little?* Write **generously** on the chart paper. (Allow responses.) Then **say:** *When you give generously, it means you give a lot.* ***Generously*** *is a describing word, too, but it is an adverb. Adverbs describe a verb.* ***Generously*** *describes the verb* ***to give***. Show students how to change an adjective to an adverb by adding the suffix **-ly**. Write a few examples on the chart paper: **clever/cleverly**, **infrequent/infrequently**, and **dreadful/dreadfully**. Ask students to share a few other adjectives and adverbs. Write their ideas on the chart paper.

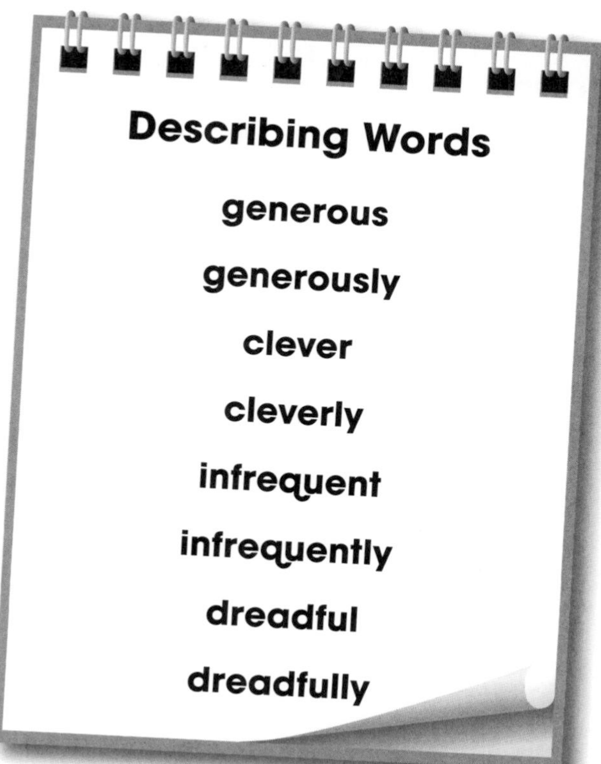

- Hand out the Day 1 activity page. Read aloud the directions and the first sentence. **Say:** *Adding the suffix* ***-ly*** *to the adjective* ***bold*** *makes it the adverb* ***boldly****. Write* ***boldly*** *on the line. I know that* ***bold*** *means "confident," so* ***boldly*** *must mean "to act with confidence." Draw a line to the definition.* **Ask:** *If I subtract* ***-ly*** *from the adverb* ***courageously****, what adjective does it become?* (Allow responses.) Then **say:** ***Courageously*** *becomes the adjective* ***courageous****. Write* ***courageous*** *on the line.* ***Courageous*** *means "brave." Draw a line to* ***brave****.* Continue to guide students as needed.

Name ______________________________

Adjective and Adverb Addition and Subtraction

Add the suffix *-ly* to create an adverb. Subtract it to create an adjective. Write the new word on the line. Draw a line to each new word's definition.

bold + ly = ______________________	**to act with confidence**
courageously - ly = ______________________	**to act with good manners**
randomly - ly = ______________________	**to behave in a way that can cause harm**
dangerous + ly = ______________________	**brave**
kind + ly = ______________________	**no order or purpose**
hastily - ly = ______________________	**not long ago**
polite + ly = ______________________	**quick**
recently - ly = ______________________	**thoughtful**

Name ____________________

Describing Word Identification

Read the sentences. Find the describing word in each sentence. Draw a circle around adjectives. Underline adverbs. Then find the words in the Word Find below.

The absorbent sponge soaked up all the water.

The dancer leaped gracefully into the air.

The principal spoke gravely to the class about their misbehavior.

It is irresponsible to litter.

An optimistic person always sees the good in everything.

The woman generously donated her time to help the sick children.

We look both ways and then cross the street cautiously.

This irritating rash is very itchy.

Word Find

T	X	O	P	L	V	B	O	W	E	N	O	A	M	O	U	S
O	P	T	I	M	I	S	T	I	C	A	C	B	S	G	V	G
N	S	C	Z	B	N	Y	K	L	J	R	A	S	X	R	X	R
C	A	U	T	I	O	U	S	L	Y	O	U	O	X	A	L	A
T	M	P	O	N	H	V	H	M	L	P	T	R	P	C	U	V
E	D	I	R	R	E	S	P	O	N	S	I	B	L	E	M	E
Y	O	P	E	R	F	H	Y	C	B	J	O	E	E	F	B	L
D	E	S	A	Q	D	O	P	E	A	C	U	N	U	U	O	Y
I	R	R	I	T	A	T	I	N	G	P	S	T	R	L	E	Y
O	P	E	R	F	H	G	E	N	E	R	O	U	S	L	Y	R
N	S	C	Z	B	N	Y	K	L	J	R	Y	R	X	Y	A	R

Name ______________________________

Cloze It Up!

Read each sentence. Draw a circle around the adjective or adverb that best completes it. Write the word on the line.

Your test score is ______________________, but it could be better if you study harder. **acceptably** **acceptable**

The dog came ______________________ close to being hit by a car.
dangerous **dangerously**

The doctor spoke ______________________ about the sick man's illness.
gravely **grave**

The happy baby slept ______________________.
peacefully **peaceful**

The ______________________ child finished her homework.
responsible **responsibly**

In the summer, my family makes ______________________ visits to the ice cream shop. **frequently** **frequent**

The teacher ______________________ selects children to feed the class pets. **randomly** **random**

The police officer gave the woman a ticket for parking ______________________.
illegal **illegally**

Name ______________________________

Crossword Puzzle

Read the clues. Find the answers in the word box. Write the answers in the crossword puzzle.

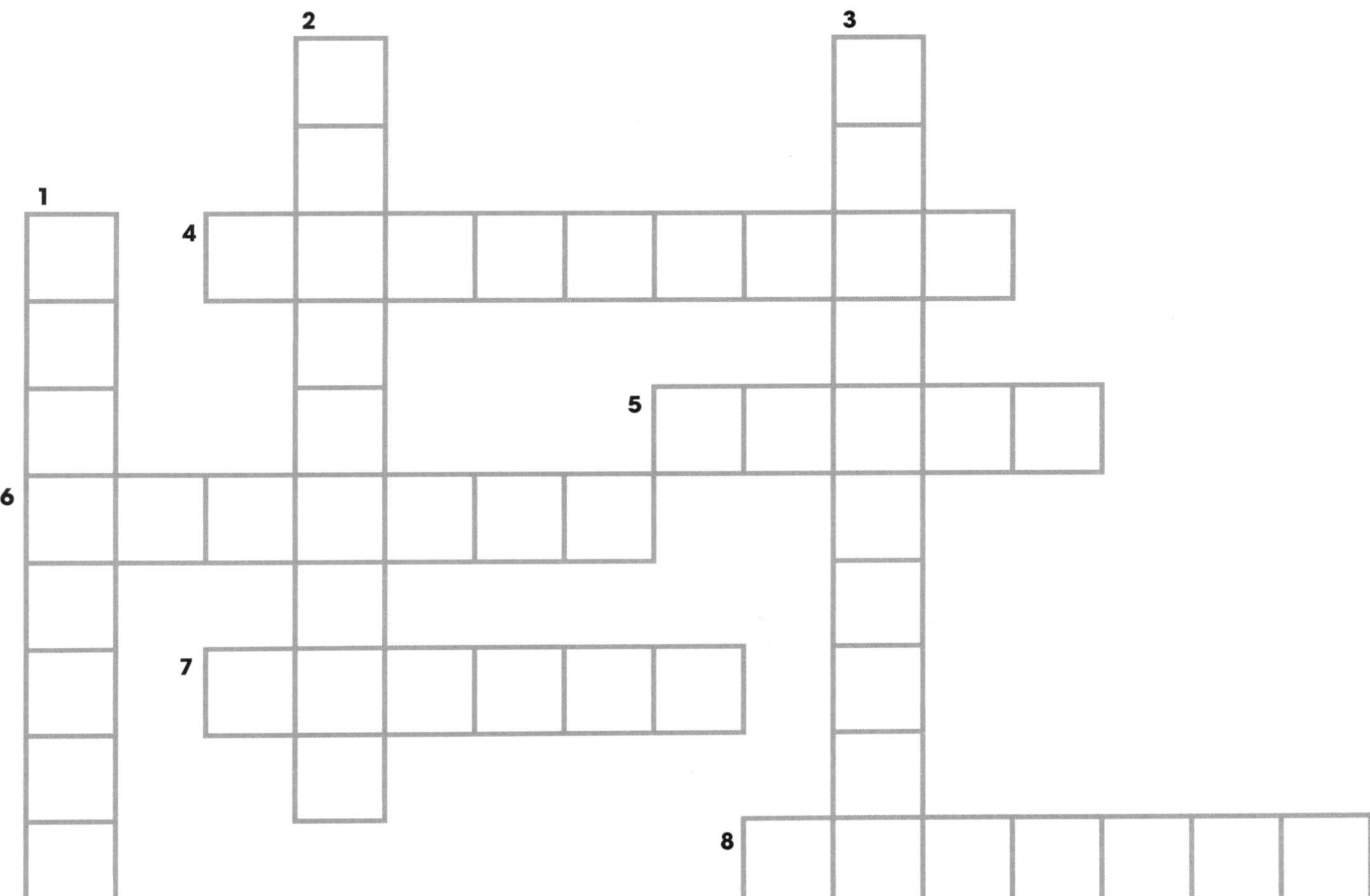

blind
cautiously
delicious
dynamic
outraged
radiant
skeptical
varied

Clues

Down

1. angry
2. having doubt
3. carefully

Across

4. tasty
5. without sight
6. shining brightly
7. not all the same
8. having a lot of energy

 Name ____________________

Assessment

Find the missing word for each sentence in the word box. Write it on the line. Identify the missing word as an adverb or adjective by checking the column.

cautiously	**clever**	**frequently**	**generous**
hastily	**optimistic**	**responsible**	

	Adverb	Adjective
To give money to charity is a(n) ____________ act.	❑	❑
The ____________ child makes her bed and cleans her dishes without being asked.	❑	❑
To do something often means to do it ____________.	❑	❑
If you are ____________, you have a quick mind.	❑	❑
When you do something ____________, you do it quickly and without care.	❑	❑
If you see the bright side of a situation, you are a(n) ____________ person.	❑	❑
To do something carefully, you do it ____________.	❑	❑

Overview Prefixes and Suffixes

Directions and Sample Answers for Activity Pages

Day 1	See "Provide a Real-World Example" below.
Day 2	Read aloud the title and directions. Help students cut out and read the words. Point out that each prefix stands for a number. Help students glue the words in the correct section.
Day 3	Read aloud the title and directions. Help students identify and draw a circle around the word or words that correctly complete each sentence.
Day 4	Read aloud the title and directions. Help students read the clues and find answers in the word box. Model how to write a word into the crossword puzzle.
Day 5	Read aloud the directions. Allow time for students to complete the task. Afterward, meet individually with students to discuss their results. Use their responses to plan further instruction and review.

Provide a Real-World Example

- Display an empty water bottle. **Ask:** *When we finish drinking water, what can we do with the empty water bottle?* (Allow responses.) *We can recycle, or use the bottle again. The prefix* ***re-*** *means "to do again." So if we refill the empty bottle with water, we are filling it again. Knowing the meaning of a prefix helps us figure out unknown words.* Write **recycle** and **refill** on chart paper or the board.
- **Say:** *Knowing the meaning of a suffix can also help us figure out an unknown word. What do we call someone who acts in plays?* (Allow responses.) *We call that person an actor. The suffix* ***-or*** *is a clue. Knowing that* ***-or*** *means a person who takes part in something or does something helps us know that an actor is a person who acts.* Write **actor** on the chart paper. Then **say:** *Brad Pitt is a famous actor. What do you think* ***famous*** *means?* (Allow responses.) *The suffix* ***-ous*** *means "to be full of" or "to have," so* ***famous*** *means "to have lots of fame."* Write **famous** on the chart paper.

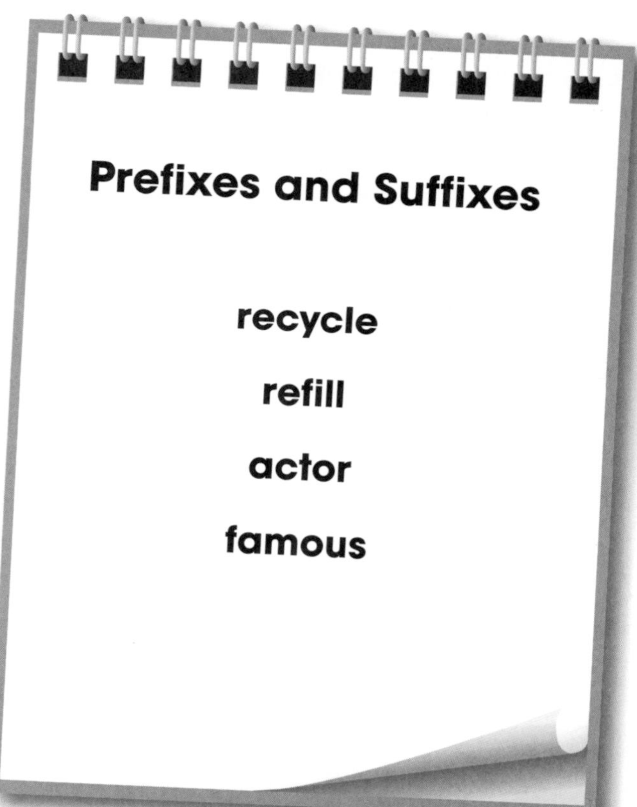

- Hand out the Day 1 activity page. Read aloud the directions and the first prefix and sample word. **Say:** *I know the word* ***impossible*** *means that something is not possible or able to be done, so the prefix* ***im-*** *must mean "not." Draw a line to* ***not***. Focus on the next item. **Say:** *I see the word* ***move*** *in the word* ***movement****. I know* ***move*** *is a verb. Adding the suffix* ***-ment*** *changes the verb to a noun. So* ***-ment*** *is a suffix that makes a word a noun. Draw a line to this definition.* Continue to guide students as needed.

Prefix and Suffix Match-Up

Match prefixes and suffixes to their meaning or their function on the right. Draw a line to make a match. The words in parentheses are clues to help you identify the meaning of the prefix or suffix.

im- (impossible)	**again**
-ment (movement)	**before**
pre- (preview)	**forms a noun**
bi- (bicycle)	**not**
-ive (active)	**person who does something**
co- (coworker)	**two**
-ist (dentist)	**with**
re- (reproduce)	**forms an adjective**

Name ____________________

How Many?

Cut out the words. Glue each one in the correct box.

One	Two	Three	Four	Eight

bicycle	octopus	quadruplets	triangle	unicycle
bifocals	octagon	quadrilateral	unicorn	tricycle
unify	quadratic	triathlon	bilingual	octet

Cloze It Up!

Read each sentence. Draw a circle around the word or words that best complete it.

A biweekly newspaper comes out **three/two** times each week.

If you preview a movie, you see it **before/after** it comes out.

A toxic substance is one that **has/has no** toxins, or poison.

An educator is a person who **educates/does not educated**.

An independent person is one who **is/is not** dependent on others.

A unicycle has **two wheels/one wheel**.

A persuasive politician is one who **easily convinces/is easily convinced**.

If I renew the library book, I **return it/keep it**.

An internal organ is one that is **outside/inside** your body.

 Name ______________________________

Crossword Puzzle

Read the clues. Find the answers in the word box. Write the answers in the crossword puzzle.

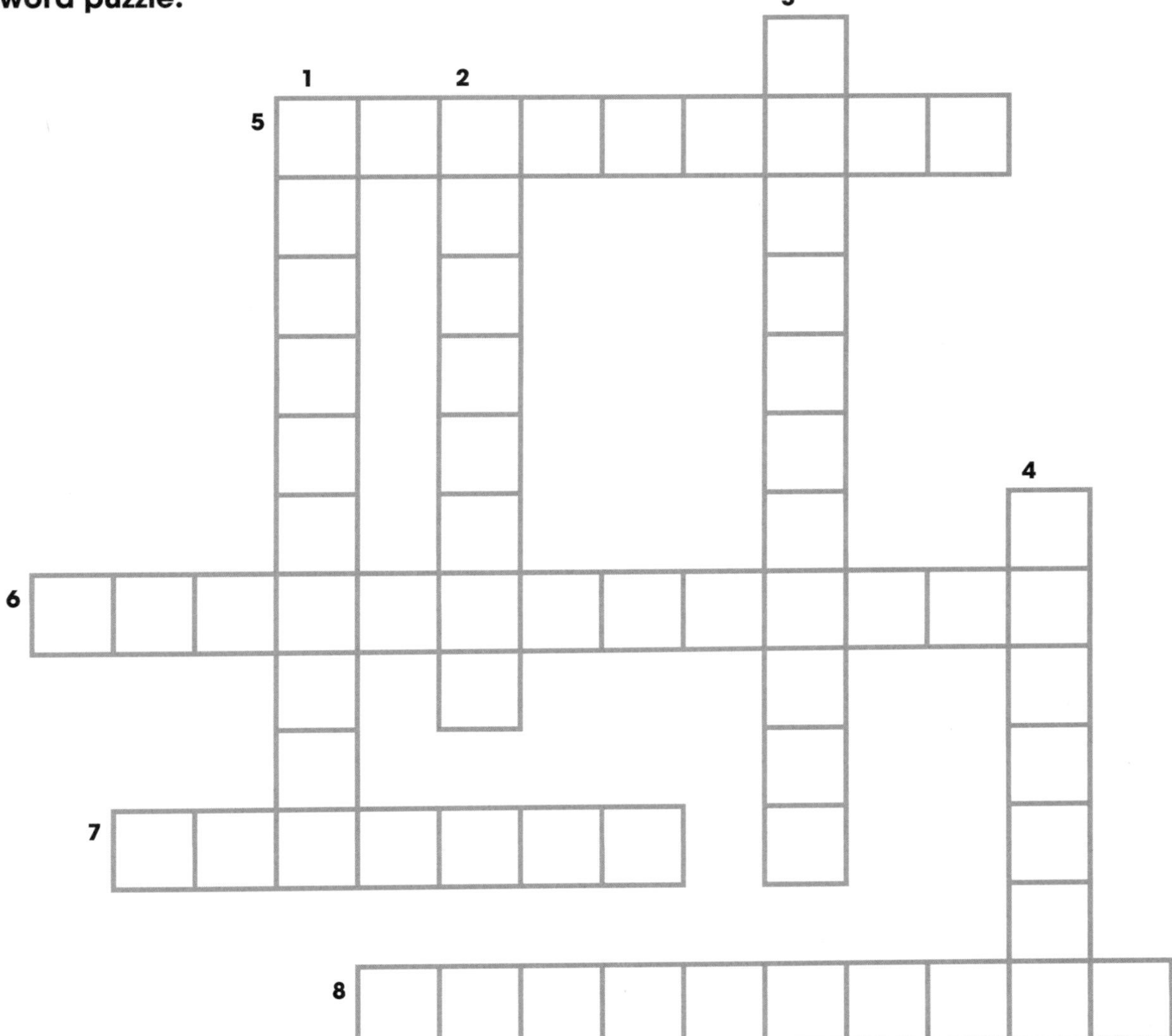

appearance
coexist
colonist
dynamic
illiterate
incorrect
reconstruct
untrustworthy

Clues

Down

1. not able to read or write
2. person who lives in a newly settled area
3. to build again
4. energetic

Across

5. not right
6. not reliable
7. to live together
8. how something or someone looks

Assessment

Find the missing word for each sentence in the word box. Write it on the line.

active	**coworkers**	**educator**
preview	**quadrilateral**	**rebuild**

When you ____________________ a book, you read about it before you buy it.

A(n) ____________________ is a shape with four sides and four angles.

Two people working in the same office are ____________________.

The ____________________ toddler was on the move all day long!

A teacher is a(n) ____________________.

The family plans to ____________________ their house that burned down.

Overview Roots and Compound Words

Directions and Sample Answers for Activity Pages

Day 1	See "Provide a Real-World Example" below.
Day 2	Read aloud the title and directions. Cut out one set of words for the class to use. Fold the words and have each student choose one. Guide them to find a classmate who has the other half of their compound word. Remind pairs to define the word and use it in a sentence.
Day 3	Read aloud the title and directions. Help students identify and underline the word that correctly completes each sentence. Guide them to draw a circle around the root.
Day 4	Read aloud the title and directions. Help students read the clues and find answers in the word box. Model how to write a word into the crossword puzzle.
Day 5	Read aloud the directions. Allow time for students to complete the task. Afterward, meet individually with students to discuss their results. Use their responses to plan further instruction and review.

Provide a Real-World Example

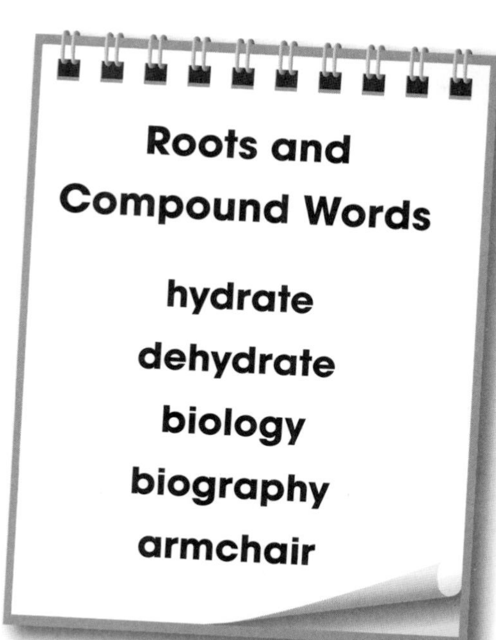

- Fill a glass with water and drink it. **Say:** *Aaah! Now I am hydrated. What do you think* ***hydrate*** *means?* (Allow responses.) Then **say:** ***Hydrate*** *means "to have water." The root or basic part of the word is* ***hydro****, which means "water." So if a person is dehydrated, what does it mean?* (Allow responses.) Then **say:** *When you add the prefix* ***de-*** *to* ***hydrate****, it has the opposite meaning: to remove water from.* Write **hydrate** and **dehydrate** on chart paper or the board.

- **Say:** *Some words are made up of a root word and a suffix. For example, the word* ***biology*** *includes the root* ***bio****, meaning "life," and the suffix* ***-logy****, meaning "the study of." So biology is the study of life.* Write **biology** on the chart paper. Ask students what biographies they've read. **Ask:** *What kind of book is a biography?* (Allow responses.) ***Biography*** *is a word that has two roots:* ***bio*** *and* ***graph****. Remember,* ***bio*** *means "life" and* ***graph*** *means "writing" or "printing," so a biography is a book about a person's life.* Write **biography** on the chart paper.

- Point out that a compound word is different than the other examples because it is made up of two words that can stand on their own. Give an example, such as **armchair**. Ask students to identify the two words in **armchair**. Write **armchair** on the chart paper.

- Hand out the Day 1 activity page. Read aloud the directions and the first root and sample word. **Say:** *I know* ***annual*** *means that something happens every year, so the root* ***ann-*** *must mean "year." Draw a line to* ***year****.* Focus on the next item. **Say:** *I know that when we studied geology, we learned about Earth. If geology is the study of Earth, then* ***geo*** *must mean "earth." Draw a line to* ***earth****.* Continue to guide students as needed.

 Name ______________________________

Root Match-Up

Draw a line to match each root to its meaning. The words in parentheses are clues to help you identify the meaning of the roots.

ann- (annual)	**earth**
geo- (geology)	**heat**
aud- (audio)	**letter**
carn- (carnivore)	**look**
chron- (chronicle)	**year**
-crat (autocrat)	**sound**
liter- (literature)	**time**
spec- (spectator)	**meat**
therm- (thermometer)	**ruler**

Name ____________________________

Make-a-Word

Cut out the words, fold them, and put them in a container. Pick a word. Find the person whose word with your word creates a compound word. Together, define the word and use it in a sentence.

air	brush	base	ball	bed
spread	table	cloth	fresh	water
salt	water	out	grow	over
grown	under	ground	up	beat
up	date	stead	fast	corner
stone	back	yard	down	stairs

Name ______________________________

Cloze It Up!

Read each sentence. Underline the word that best completes it. Draw a circle around the root.

Our wedding **annual/anniversary** is the first of May.

Time lines show events in **chronological/chronicle** order.

The **carnival/carnivorous** lion attacked and ate the zebra.

First you **combine/complete** the ingredients and then you stir them.

In a **democracy/epidemic**, citizens vote for their leaders.

The combination of **hydrogen/hydrate** and oxygen forms water.

Literature/Literate includes plays, stories, and poetry.

The **spectacles/spectators** clapped when their team scored a goal.

I keep my soup warm in a **thermos/thermometer**.

The **zoology/zoologist** visited our class and taught us about animals.

 Name ______________________

Crossword Puzzle

Read the clues. Find the answers in the word box. Write the answers in the crossword puzzle.

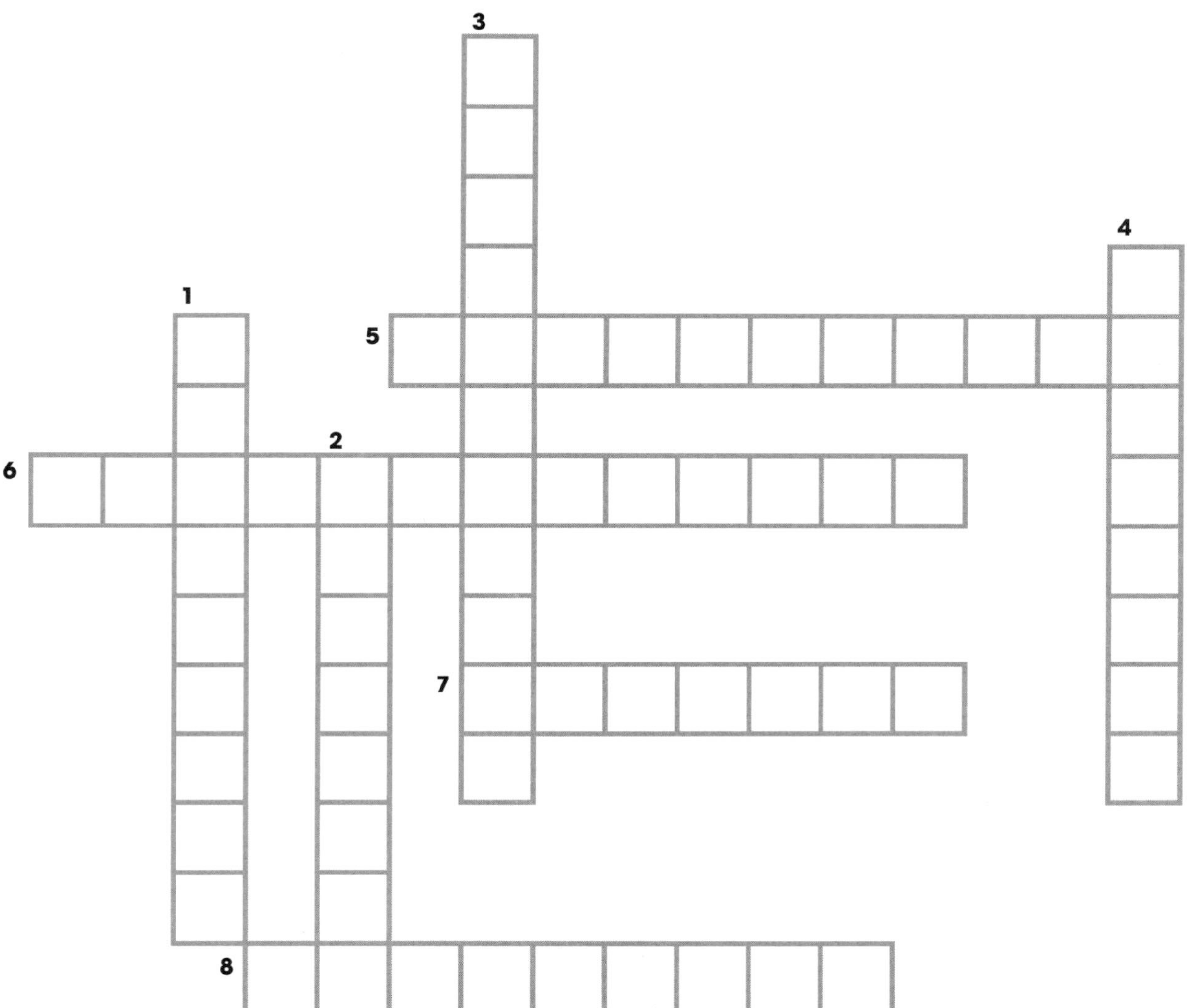

autobiography
biennial
clockwise
credible
literally
synchronize
thermometer
zoology

Clues

Down

1. word for word
2. happening every two years
3. to happen at the same time
4. believable

Across

5. instrument that measures temperature
6. the story of one's own life
7. study of animals
8. in the direction that the hands of a clock move

Assessment

Find the missing word for each sentence in the word box. Write it on the line.

annual	**chronicle**	**geology**
hydrate	**thermometer**	**underground**

The roots of a tree grow ____________________.

I used a ____________________ to check the sick child's temperature.

Be sure to ____________________ on hot summer days.

Valentine's Day is a(n) ____________________ holiday.

Journalists ____________________ events in the order that they happen.

In ____________________, we learn about Earth's layers of soil and rock.

Overview Synonyms and Antonyms

Directions and Sample Answers for Activity Pages

Day 1	See "Provide a Real-World Example" below.
Day 2	Read aloud the title and directions. Help students read the sentences. Remind them that synonyms are words that have the same or almost the same meaning. Guide them to find a synonym for each underlined word and write it on the line.
Day 3	Read aloud the title and directions. Remind students that antonyms are words with opposite meanings. Help them find the two words in each sentence that are antonyms and draw a circle around them.
Day 4	Read aloud the title and directions. Divide the class into pairs. Guide pairs to choose a game board. Remind them that when marking X or O, they also write a synonym or antonym. Have pairs share their antonyms and synonyms with the rest of the class after they play.
Day 5	Read aloud the directions. Allow time for students to complete the task. Afterward, meet individually with students to discuss their results. Use their responses to plan further instruction and review.

Provide a Real-World Example

- Stand in front of the class and rub your stomach. **Say:** *I am starving!* Write **starving** on the chart paper or the board. Ask students what words mean the same as **starving**. Write students' responses on the chart paper under the heading "Synonyms." **Say:** *Words with the same or almost the same meaning are called synonyms. Some synonyms for starving are **hungry** and **famished**.* Write **hungry** and **famished** on the chart paper.

- Now **say:** *When you do feel hungry, I encourage you to eat healthy food. I discourage you from eating junk food.* Write **encourage** and **discourage** on the chart paper under the heading "Antonyms." Invite students to suggest what these words mean. Then **say:** ***Encourage** means to support someone to do something, and **discourage** means to convince or persuade someone not to do something. The prefix **dis-** means "not" and is a clue that **discourage** is the opposite of **encourage**. Words that have opposite meanings, such as **encourage** and **discourage**, are called antonyms.*

- Hand out the Day 1 activity page. Read aloud the title and directions. Then read the first word pair. **Say:** ***Agree** means to have the same opinion or feel the same way as someone else. When I disagree with someone, it means I do not have the same opinion or feel the same way. These words are opposites, or antonyms. Check the "Antonym" box.* Read aloud the second word pair. **Say:** *Generous people give their time and/or money to help others. So **generous** and **giving** must mean the same thing. Check the "Synonym" box.*

Name ______________________________

Check It!

Read each word pair. Check the "Antonym" or "Synonym" box.

	Antonym	Synonym
agree/disagree	❑	❑
generous/giving	❑	❑
fade/discolor	❑	❑
increase/decrease	❑	❑
protect/harm	❑	❑
allow/prohibit	❑	❑
confess/admit	❑	❑
comprehend/understand	❑	❑
flavorful/zesty	❑	❑
repair/damage	❑	❑

Name ______________________________

Synonym Search

Read each sentence. Find a synonym for the underlined word in the word box. Write it on the line.

adapt	bother	courageous	dampen	demand
examine	frigid	happy	recall	show

"Don't pester your sister," said Mom. ______________________

Some animals change to survive in their habitat. ______________________

If you moisten the glue on an envelope, it will stick. ______________________

The shop owner put the dress on display in the window. ______________________

We can study the tiny insect under a microscope. ______________________

I do not like the cold winter air. ______________________

The baby was content after I fed her. ______________________

I find it hard to remember people's names. ______________________

My parents insist that I wash my hands before I eat. ______________________

The brave firefighter ran into the burning house. ______________________

Name ______________________________

Antonyms, Antonyms Everywhere

Read each sentence. Draw circles around the antonyms.

The race began in town and concluded in the park.

First separate the eggs, and then combine the yolks with the sugar.

Jill accepts one invitation but declines another.

I deposit my check into my savings account and withdraw a little spending money.

As the clouds appeared, the sun disappeared.

Sometimes you need to fail before you can succeed.

I forgot to buy milk, but I remembered to buy orange juice.

My dependable fan kept me cool after my unreliable air conditioner broke.

The responsible student studied, while the irresponsible one watched TV.

I admire the actor but detest the movie.

Name ______________________________

Tic-Tac-Toe

Play with a partner. Choose a tic-tac-toe board and read aloud the word at the top. The first player marks an X in a space and writes a synonym for the word. The next player marks a space with an O and writes an antonym for the word. Play until someone gets three in a row.

admire

bold

persuade

reveal

 Name ____________________

Assessment

Color the stars with antonyms red. Color the stars with synonyms blue. Then write an antonym for the word *reveal* in one star a synonym for the word *bold* in the other.

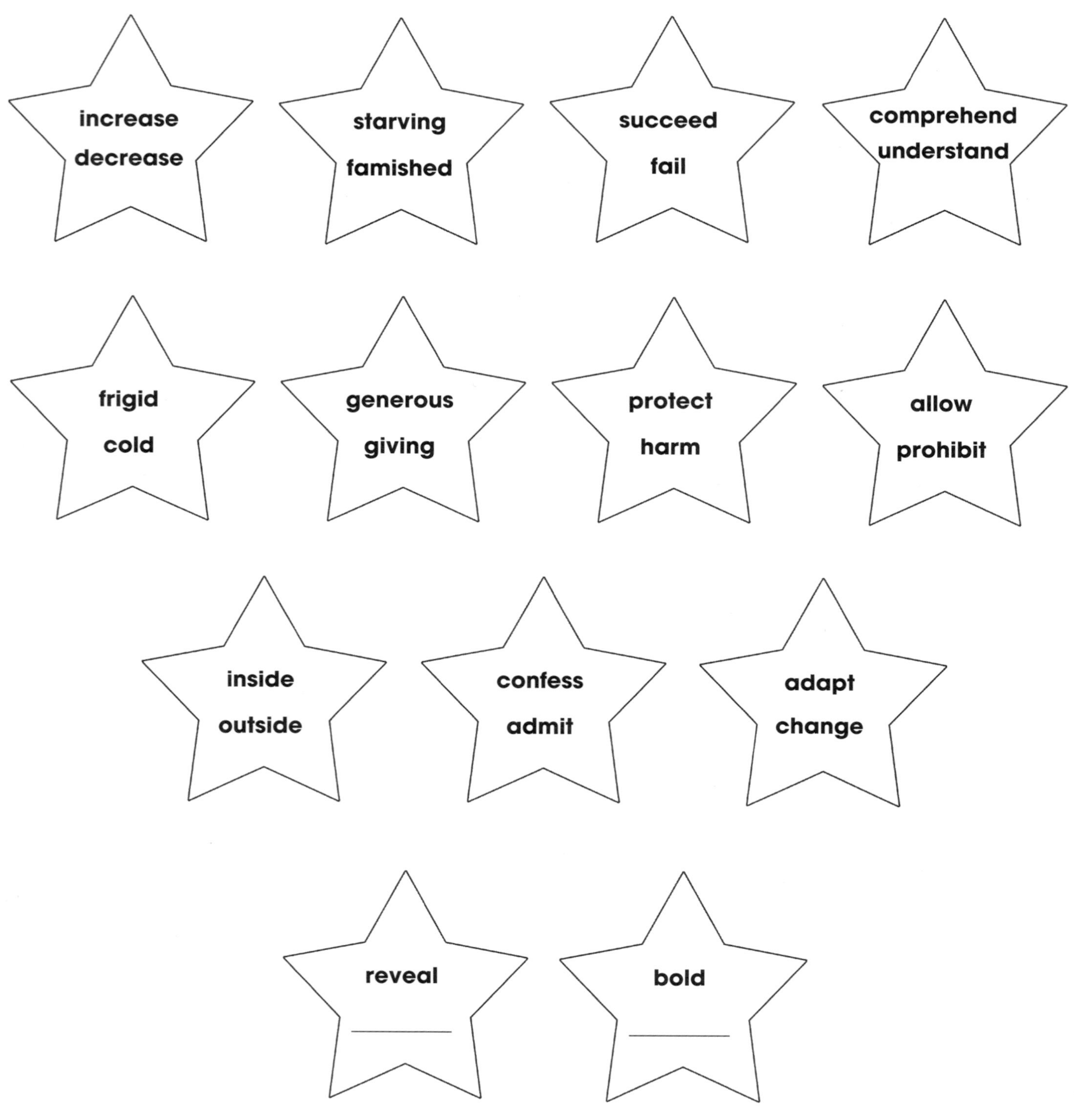

Overview Multiple-Meaning Words

Directions and Sample Answers for Activity Pages

Day 1	See "Provide a Real-World Example" below.
Day 2	Read aloud the title and directions. Help students read the sentences, focusing on the underlined words. Guide them to draw a line matching each sentence with a definition of the underlined word.
Day 3	Read aloud the title and directions. Help students read each sentence and identify the homonym that correctly completes it. Help them write the word on the line. (effect, cell, dye, earn, phase, kernel, yolk, soared, cellar, profit)
Day 4	Read aloud the title and directions. Help students cut out and glue words onto their Bingo cards. Cut out a set of words for yourself, fold them, and put them in a container. As you pick each word, use it in a sentence so students have context and know which word you are referring to. For example, you might say, "The chair is made of metal."
Day 5	Read aloud the directions. Allow time for students to complete the first task. Then read aloud this sentence: *I water my plant every day.* Have students draw a picture. Afterward, meet individually with students to discuss their results. Use their responses to plan further instruction and review.

Provide a Real-World Example

- **Say:** *I rode my bicycle on the road. Which word did you hear twice?* (Allow responses.) Then **say:** *I rode my bicycle . . .* Write **rode** on chart paper or the board. Then **say:** *. . . on the road.* Write **road** on the chart paper. As you point to each word, **say:** ***Rode** and **road** sound the same, but we spell them differently and they have different meanings. **Rode** and **road** are homophones.*

- Write this sentence on the board as you **say:** *John waves to his children swimming in the waves.* Point to the first **waves** in this sentence. Explain that John waves his hand, so this **wave** is a verb. Model how you wave your hand. Now point to the other **waves**. **Say:** *The children are playing in ocean waves. This **wave** is a noun. **Waves** and **waves** are homonyms, or words that are spelled the same way but have different meanings.*

- Hand out the Day 1 activity page. Read aloud the title and directions. Direct students to the first picture. **Say:** *This is a penny, or cent. We spell **cent** c-e-n-t. The word **scent**, spelled s-c-e-n-t, means a "smell" or "odor." Draw a circle around **cent**.* Repeat these steps for each picture, or if students are ready, they may work independently.

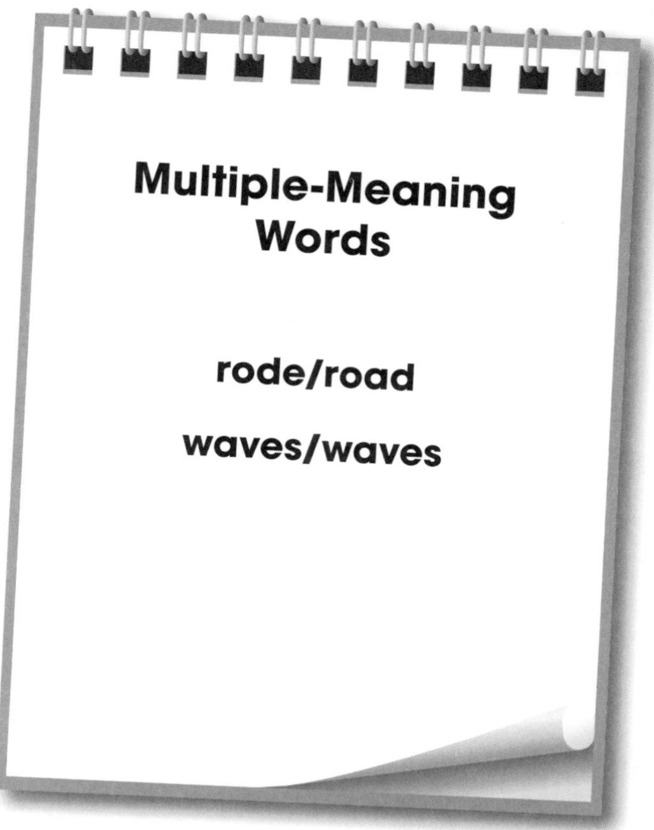

Name ______________________________

Picturing Homophones

Draw a circle around the word that matches the picture.

cent **scent**

steak **stake**

rode **rowed**

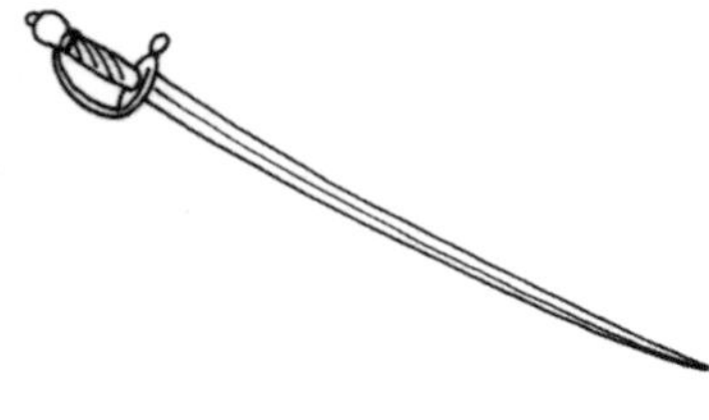

sword **soared**

hymn **him**

rays **raise**

Homonym Make-a-Match

Read each sentence. Look at the underlined word. Draw a line from each sentence to the definition of the underlined word.

The mean dog barked at the children.	to put a seed into the soil so that it can grow
The woman wore a cast on her broken leg.	unfriendly
The little plant grew fast.	to deposit or put forth
Intermission is after the second act.	a living thing that grows from the ground
I visited the grave at the cemetery.	one of the parts of a play
We won by just one point!	a place where a dead person is buried
I didn't mean to hang up on you.	very serious
I cast my ballot during the recent election.	a unit for scoring in a game
I plant vegetables in the spring.	to perform
I like to act in plays.	hard covering that supports a broken arm or leg
His serious tone let me know this was a grave matter.	sharp end of something
If you get poked by a pencil point, it hurts.	to intend to do something

Name ______________________________

Circle It!

Read each sentence. Draw a circle around the homophone that completes the sentence. Write it on the line.

One ____________________ of the big snowstorm was that schools were closed.

affect **effect**

The prisoner's ________________________ is very small.

sell **cell**

Let's ________________________ our T-shirts green.

die **dye**

I ________________________ money for babysitting.

earn **urn**

We are in ________________________ two of the project.

faze **phase**

The popcorn ________________________ got stuck in my teeth.

kernel **colonel**

The ________________________ is my favorite part of an egg.

yoke **yolk**

The plane ________________________ through the clouds.

soared **sword**

We store old clothes downstairs in the ________________________.

cellar **seller**

The children made a ________________________ selling lemonade.

prophet **profit**

Homophone Bingo

Cut out the words. Glue the words onto your Bingo card. Listen to your teacher use words in sentences. Make an X on the correct homophone. Three in a row wins BINGO!

	Free Space	

brood	brewed	discreet	discrete	metal	mettle
peak	peek	affect	effect	plum	plumb
die	dye	earn	urn	read	reed

Name ______________________________

Assessment

Draw a circle around the homophone that completes the sentence.

The heavy wind **affects/effects** traffic.

The children **cell/sell** cookies for the school bake sale.

We cook **stake/steak** on the grill.

We climbed to the mountain's **peak/peek**.

Listen to your teacher. Draw a picture of what your teacher says.

Overview Language Arts Content Words

Directions and Sample Answers for Activity Pages

Day 1	See "Provide a Real-World Example" below.
Day 2	Read aloud the title and directions. Help students read the words in both columns. Guide them to make matches.
Day 3	Read aloud the title and directions. Help students read the questions and answers. Guide them to draw a circle around the correct answers. (illustration, fairy tale, recycle, poem, introduction, nonfiction, exclamation point, period)
Day 4	Read aloud the title and directions. Help students read the clues and find answers in the word box. Model how to write a word into the crossword puzzle.
Day 5	Read aloud the directions. Allow time for students to complete the tasks. Afterward, meet individually with students to discuss their results. Use their responses to plan further instruction and review.

Provide a Real-World Example

- Display different things people read, including a textbook, storybook, magazine, newspaper, cartoon, letter, and sign. Ask students what these items have in common. After they respond, point out that these are all things we read. **Ask:** *What do we read to get information or facts?* (Allow responses.) Point to the newspaper and **say:** *We read newspapers and magazines to get information about what is happening in the world.* Point to the textbook and **say:** *In school, we read textbooks to learn facts in different subjects.* Write **newspaper**, **magazine**, and **textbook** on chart paper or the board. **Say:** *We read signs for information, too. Signs tell us which way to go.* Write **sign** on the chart paper.
- **Ask:** *What do we read for fun or entertainment?* Allow students to respond, and then **say:** *Cartoons are funny drawings that tell a story or joke. Cartoons make us laugh.* Write **cartoon** on the chart paper. Explain that we read storybooks for entertainment, too. Ask students to share the titles of stories they recently read. Write **storybook** on the chart paper. Hold up the letter. **Say:** *Some kinds of letters tell interesting stories or messages that are meant to entertain.* Write **letter** on the chart paper.
- Hand out the Day 1 activity page. Read aloud the title and directions. **Say:** *We read nonfiction to get information on a topic. Write **nonfiction** on the "Information" side. Some magazines feature news and others are for entertainment. Write **magazine** in the overlapping section.* Guide students through the remaining words as needed.

Name ____________________

What We Read

Read the words in the word box. Write each word in the Venn diagram in the "Information," "Entertainment," or "Both" section.

folktale	magazine	myth	nonfiction
outline	poem	story	textbook

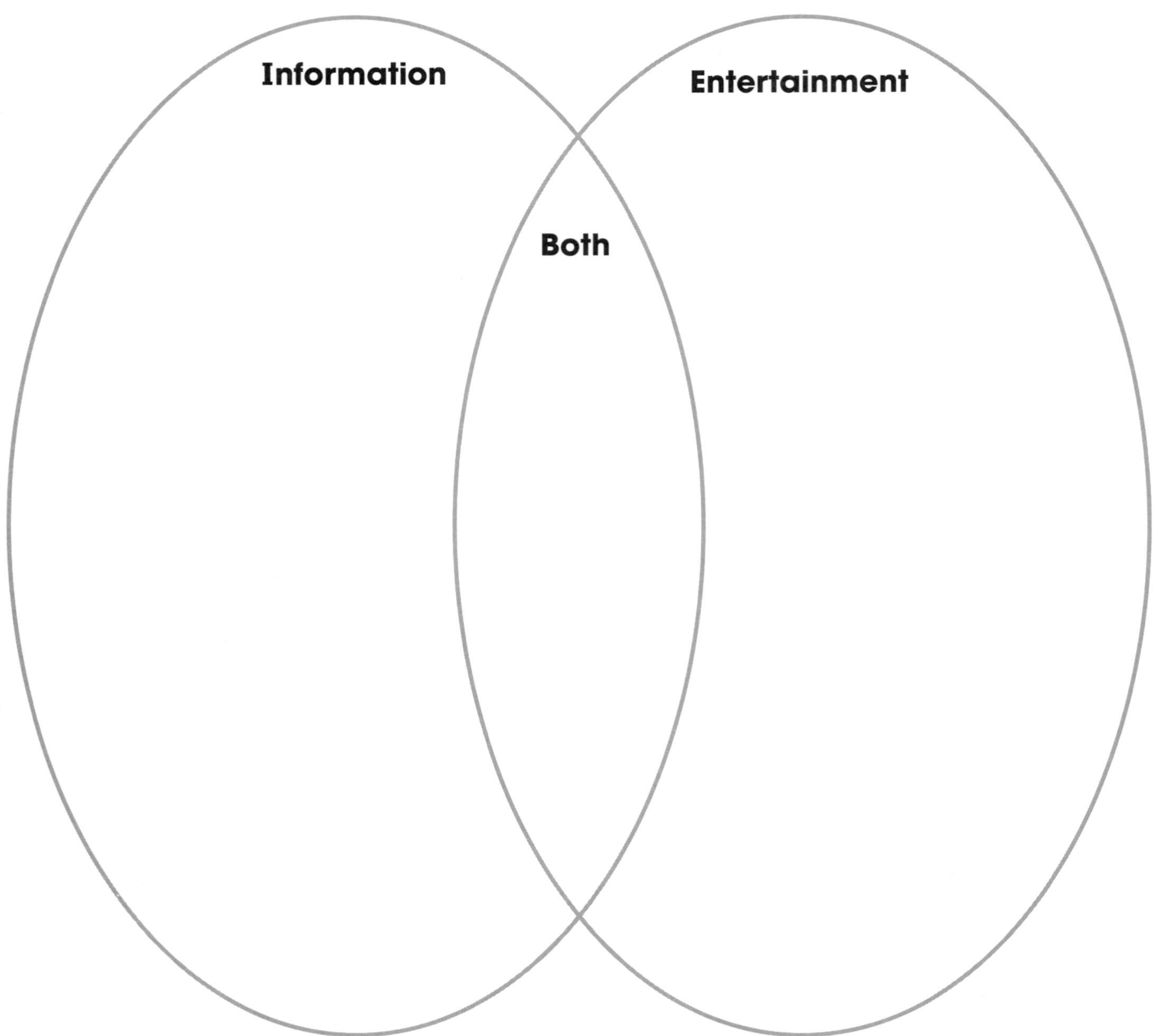

Match-Up

Draw a line to make a match.

furry cat	exclamation point
walk	consonants
Kim	colon
a, e, i, o, u	verb
apple, peaches, and grapes	adjective
Who's there?	comma
b, d, f, g, h	question mark
Stop!	uppercase
"Hello," said Mom.	quotation marks
Ingredients: eggs, flour, sugar	vowels

Which One?

Read each question. Draw a circle around the answer.

Which means the same as a drawing?	**illustration**	**photograph**	**table of contents**
Which might include a prince?	**textbook**	**newspaper**	**fairy tale**
Which word has a prefix?	**recycle**	**slowly**	**driving**
Which word is a noun?	**read**	**poem**	**sad**
Which is at the beginning of an essay?	**conclusion**	**introduction**	**climax**
Which genre is not like the others?	**nonfiction**	**myth**	**legend**
Which punctuation is for a strong feeling?	**period**	**question mark**	**exclamation point**
Which is a homograph?	**vowel**	**song**	**period**

 Name ____________________

Literary Words Crossword Puzzle

Look at the clues. Find the words in the word box. Write the answers in the crossword puzzle.

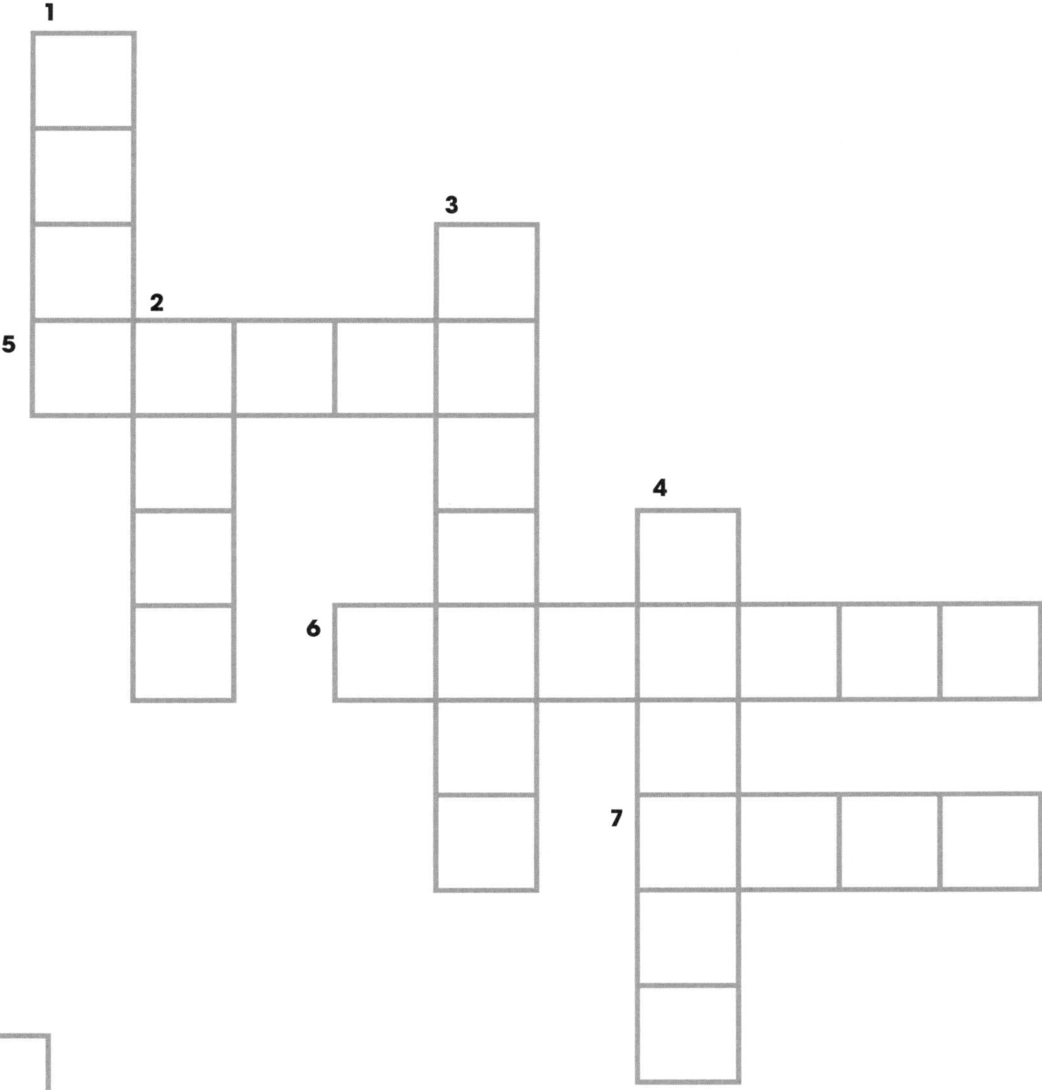

climax
hero
mood
plot
setting
theme
villain

Clues

Down

1. sequence of events in a story
2. main character
3. where a story happens
4. high point of a story

Across

5. main idea
6. evil character
7. feeling of a story

Name ______________________________

Assessment

Draw a circle around the word that correctly completes each sentence.

A villain is an example of a **character/book**.

Folktales are **fiction/nonfiction**.

We read a cartoon for **information/entertainment**.

The **climax/introduction** is the most exciting part of a story.

Sentences end with a **comma/period**.

Sentences begin with a(n) **uppercase/lowercase** letter.

Write your answer to each question on the line.

What do you read for fun?

____

What do you read for information?

____

Who is your favorite character from a book?

____

Overview Exploring the Americas and Life in the Colonies

Directions and Sample Answers for Activity Pages

Day 1	See "Provide a Real-World Example" below.
Day 2	Read aloud the title and directions. Help students read the clues and find answers in the word box. Model how to write a word into the crossword puzzle.
Day 3	Read aloud the title and directions. Read aloud the passage with students. Guide them to fill in the missing words using the words in the word box.
Day 4	Read aloud the title and directions. Read aloud the sentences with students. Guide them to circle the word that correctly completes each sentence.
Day 5	Read aloud the directions. Allow time for students to complete the tasks. Afterward, meet individually with students to discuss their results. Use their responses to plan further instruction and review.

Provide a Real-World Example

- **Say or chant the poem:** *In fourteen hundred ninety-two, Columbus sailed the ocean blue. He had three ships and left from Spain. He sailed through sunshine, wind, and rain.* **Ask:** *Who was Columbus and where was he going?* (Allow responses.) *Christopher Columbus was an explorer from Italy. The reason for his voyage, or trip, across the Atlantic Ocean was to find a route, or path, to Asia, where he hoped to trade spices for Asian silk.* Write **explorer**, **voyage**, **route**, and **trade** on chart paper or the board.
- **Say:** *As it turned out, Columbus did not land in Asia. The islands that he called the West Indies were actually part of the Americas. These two big areas of land, or continents, were about to become known as the New World.* Write **continent** on the chart paper.
- Hand out the Day 1 activity page. Read aloud the title and directions. **Say:** *I know that a continent is a big area of land. Let's write* ***continent*** *under "Places." Columbus was an explorer, so an explorer is a person. Let's write* ***explorer*** *under "People."* Continue to guide students as needed, or allow them to work independently.

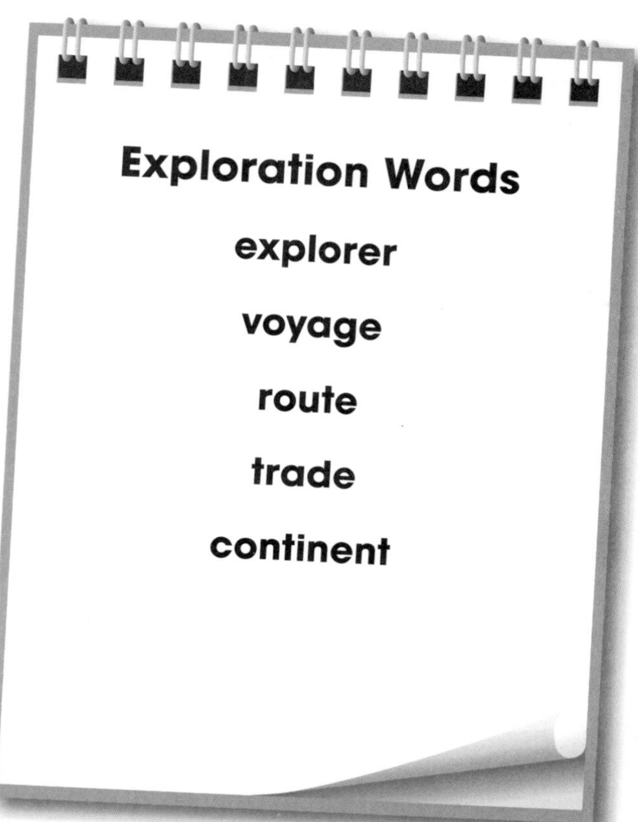

Name ______________________

People, Places, and Things

Look at the words in the word box. Write the words in the correct category on the chart.

compass	conquistador	continent	explorer
import	merchant	minerals	resources

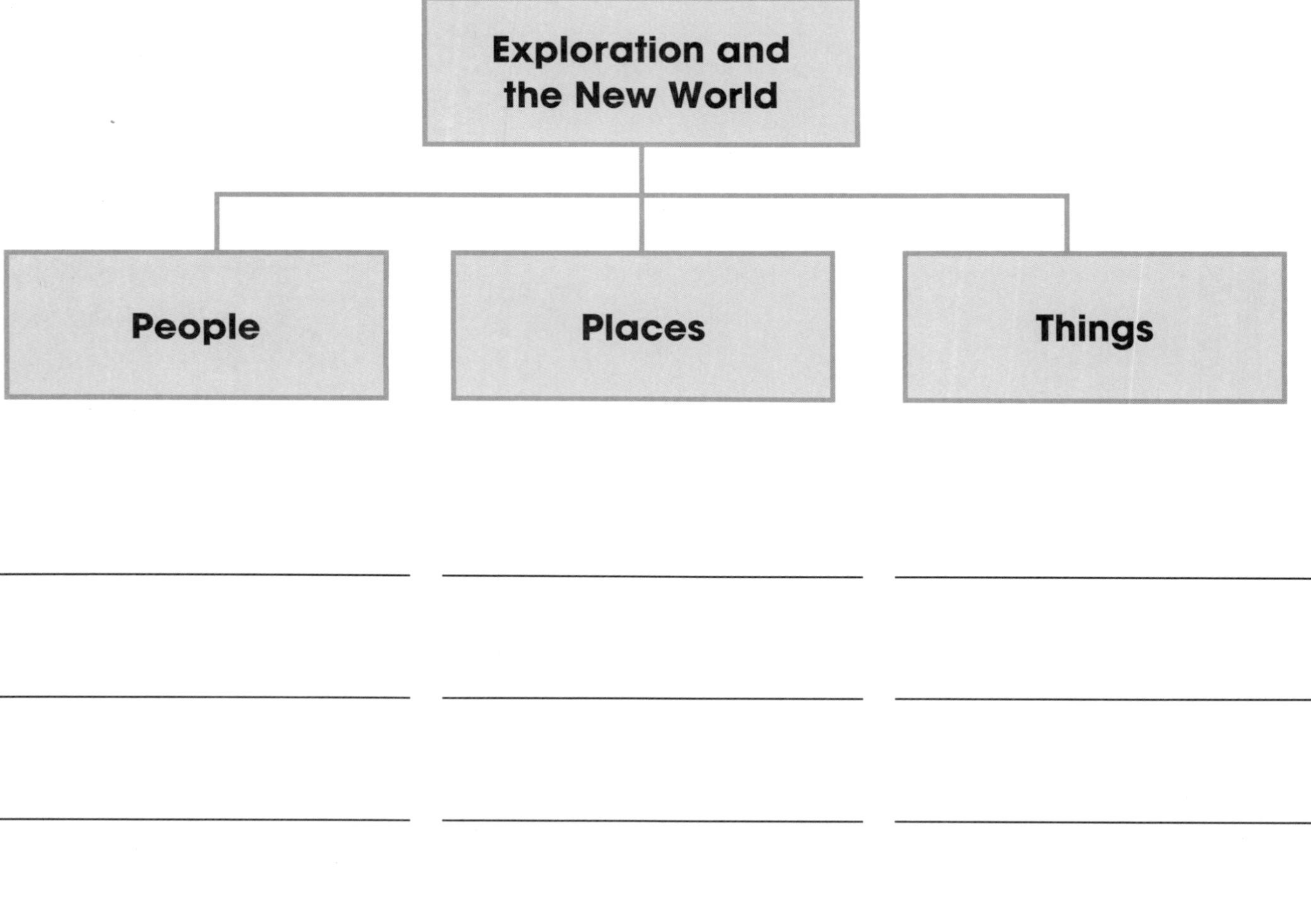

Name ____________________

Crossword Puzzle

Look at the clues. Find the words in the word box. Write the answers in the crossword puzzle.

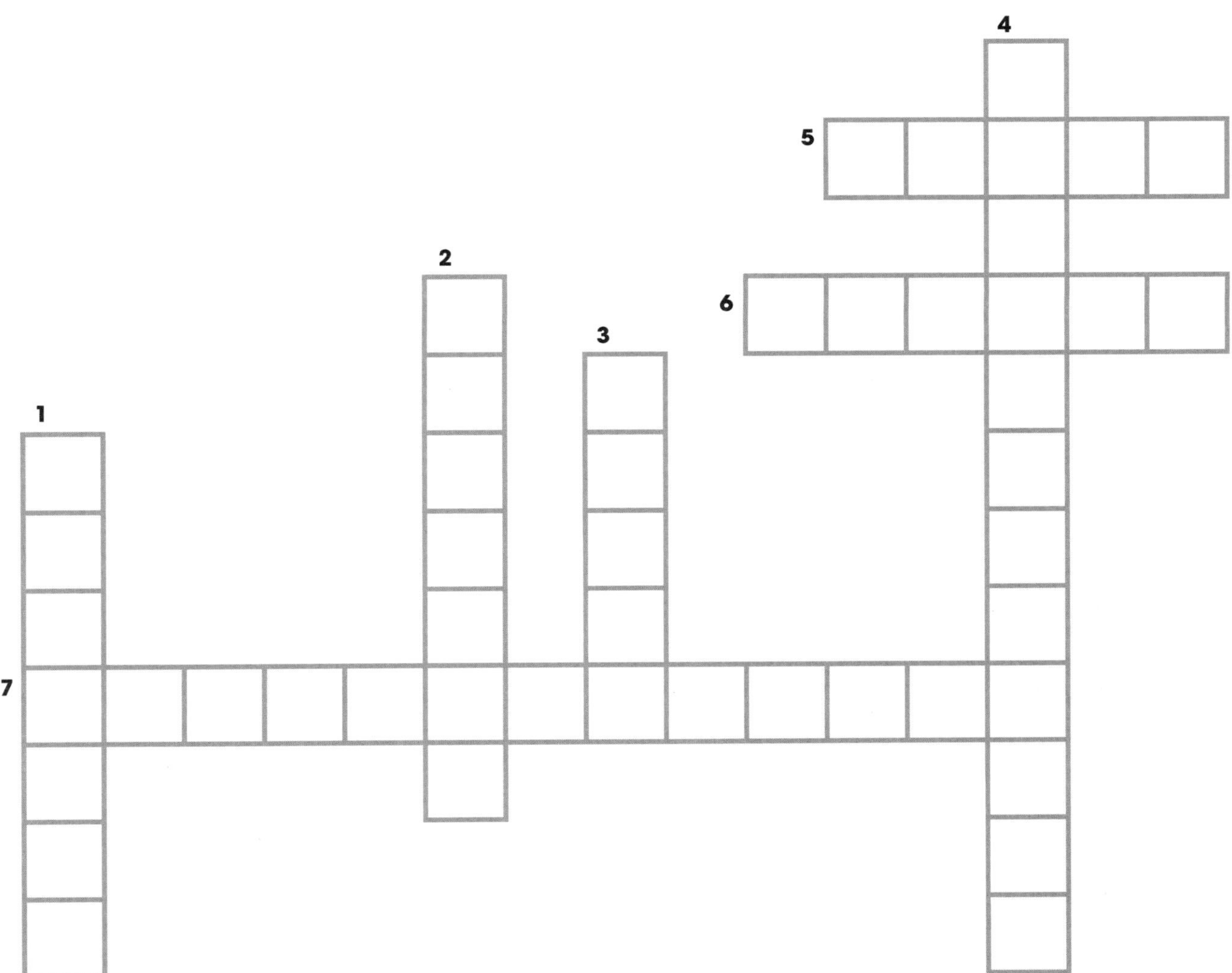

archaeologist
civilization
conquer
empire
mural
pyramid
ruins

Clues

Down

1. where an ancient king may be buried
2. take over by force
3. a painting on a wall
4. the way of life for a people

Across

5. the remains of something destroyed, such as a building
6. land and people that are ruled by a king or emperor
7. someone who studies the people of the past through the things they left behind

Name ______________________

Spanish Conquistadors

Read the passage. Write the word from the word box that best completes each sentence.

colony	**conquered**	**conquistadors**
explore	**explorers**	**nation**

The Spanish ______________________ who came after Christopher Columbus were called ______________________. These brave, tough, and often cruel men didn't just ______________________. They took land and ______________________ the people living there. By 1496, Columbus's brother had settled a ______________________ on the island of Hispaniola. From Hispaniola, the conquistadors captured the ______________________ of Cuba.

Name ______________________

Circle It!

Read the sentences. Draw a circle around the word that best completes each sentence.

The Italian navigator Amerigo Vespucci was a master at helping ships **narrate/navigate**, or find their way.

Ships loaded with New World goods returned to Spanish ports, or **houses/harbors**.

In 1519, Cuba's governor made conquistador Hernán Cortés the leader of an **expedition/exhibit**, or organized trip.

Two weeks after Ponce de León set sail from Puerto Rico, he sighted the **territory/terrace** he named Florida.

During the sixteenth and seventeenth centuries, sailors would often **mutiny/mumble**, or rebel, on the long, difficult sailing journeys.

Ships come to a **path/port** to anchor safely and load and unload goods.

Name ________________________

Assessment

Draw a line to match the words and definitions.

colony	**path**
compass	**bring into a country**
continent	**person who sells goods for profit**
import	**rebel**
mutiny	**tool for finding directions**
route	**long journey**
expedition	**one of Earth's seven large land masses**
merchant	**area settled by people from another country**

Describe a tradition in your family or at your school.

____

____

____

Overview The American Revolution

Directions and Sample Answers for Activity Pages

Day 1	See "Provide a Real-World Example" below.
Day 2	Read aloud the title and directions. Read aloud the passage with students. Guide them to fill in the missing words using the words in the word box. (colonies, Patriots, Loyalists, colonists)
Day 3	Read aloud the title and directions. Read aloud the sentences with students. Guide them to circle the word that correctly completes each sentence. (rebels, pamphlet, protest, Harbor, propaganda, tariff, Minutemen)
Day 4	Read aloud the title and directions. Help students read the clues and find answers in the word box. Model how to write a word into the crossword puzzle.
Day 5	Read aloud the directions. Allow time for students to complete the task. Afterward, meet individually with students to discuss their results. Use their responses to plan further instruction and review.

Provide a Real-World Example

- **Ask:** *How would you feel if I told you what books you could read, what shows you could watch, what food you could eat, what clothes you could wear on the weekend, or what games you could play at recess?* (Allow responses.) Then **say:** *The colonists did not like being told what to do, either. Most colonists came to the colonies precisely to have freedom. But since Britain was a monarchy, a government ruled by a king, the colonists were not free. They began to rebel against the king to win their independence. This was the beginning of the American Revolution.* Write **colonist**, **monarchy**, **rebel**, **independence**, and **revolution** on chart paper or the board.
- **Say:** *In the end, the colonists defeated the mighty British army and their dream of freedom finally came true.* Write **defeat** on the chart paper.
- Hand out the Day 1 activity page. Read aloud the title and directions. **Say:** *I know a monarchy is a kind of government where a king is the ruler. Let's write **monarchy** under "King of England." The Patriots were colonists who wanted freedom, or independence, from British rule. Let's write **independence** under "Patriots."* Continue to guide students as needed, or allow them to work independently.

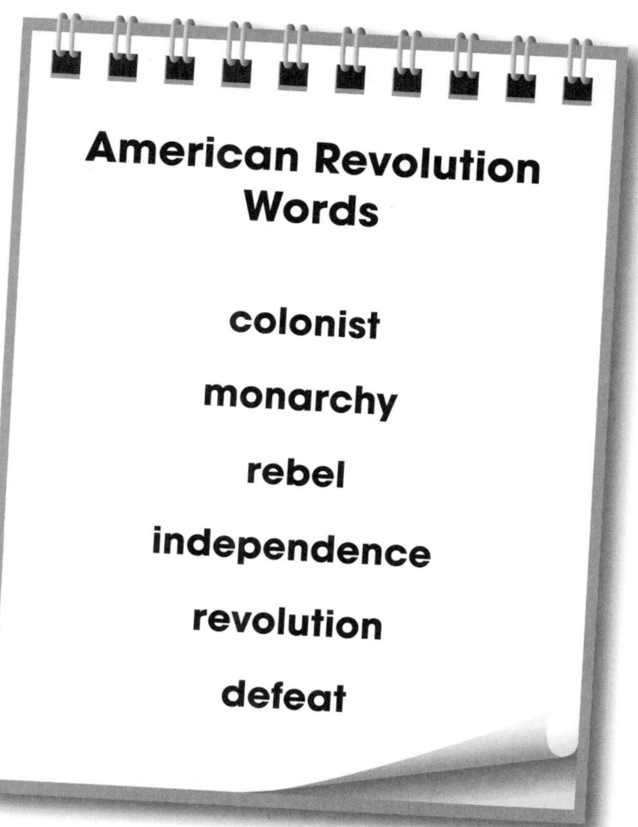

Name ______________________

King of England vs. Patriots

Write each word in the word box under "King of England" or "Patriots."

boycott	independence	Loyalist	monarchy	rebel

American Revolution

King of England	Patriots
______________________	______________________
______________________	______________________
______________________	______________________
______________________	______________________

Continental Congress

Read the passage. Write the word from the word box that best completes each sentence.

colonies	colonists
Loyalists	Patriots

In September 1774, fifty-six representatives from twelve ____________________ met at the first Continental Congress in Philadelphia. The ____________________ wanted to break from British rule. The ____________________, who supported the king, wanted the ____________________ to get along with Britain.

Circle It!

Read the sentences. Draw a circle around the word that best completes each sentence.

The colonists who did not want to obey the king's rule became known as **rebels/Loyalists**.

Many colonists read an essay, or **pact/pamphlet**, by Thomas Paine that persuaded them to break away from British rule.

To **protest/protect** Britain's Tea Act, angry colonists dumped British tea into Boston **Harbor/Sea**.

The murder of an American woman was used as **pamphlet/propaganda** against the British.

The Stamp Act forced colonists to pay a **troops/tariff** on all printed items.

Patriot troops were called **Minutemen/merchants** because they could be ready to fight very quickly.

Name ____________________

Crossword Puzzle

Look at the clues. Find the words in the word box. Write the answers in the crossword puzzle.

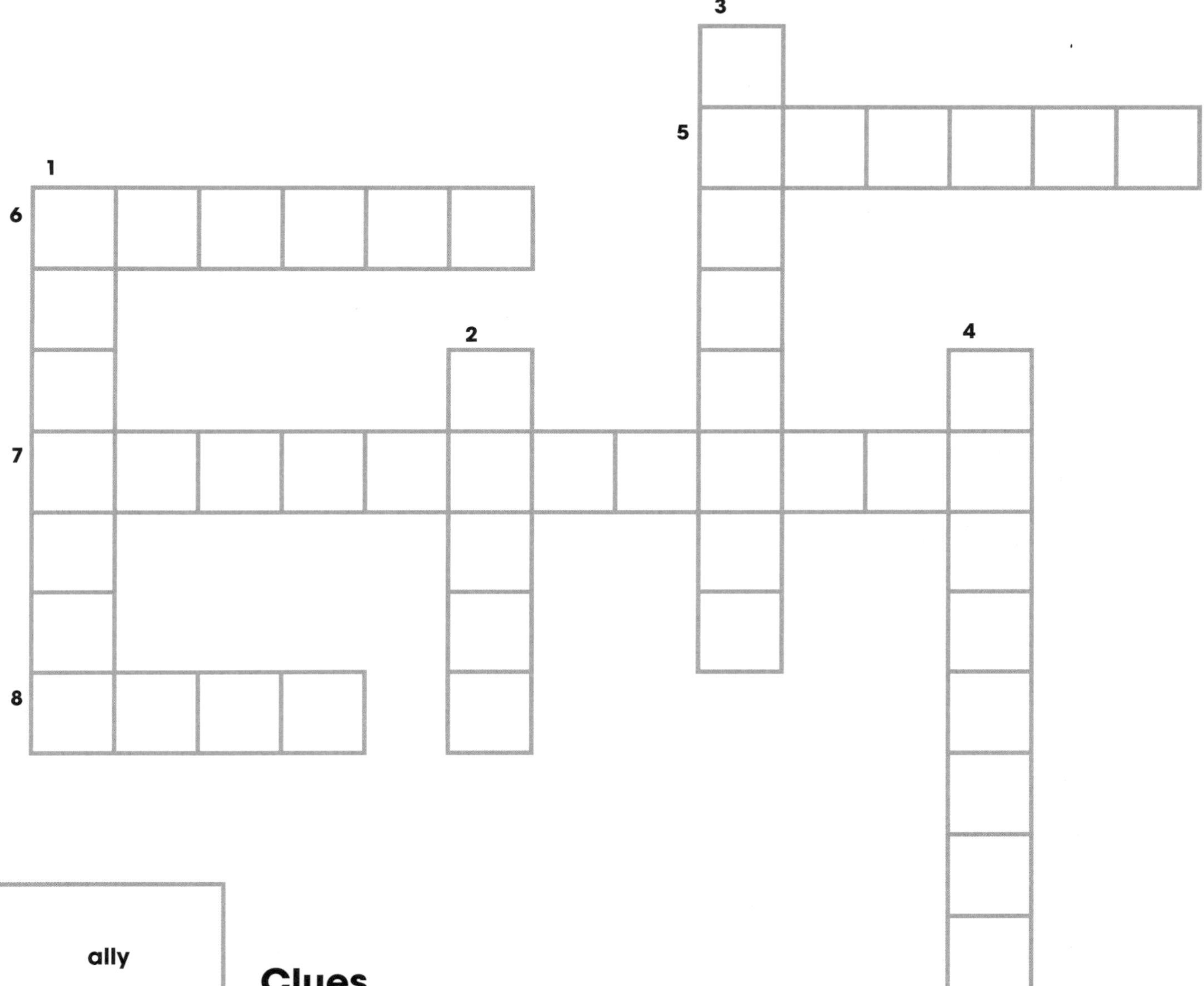

ally
independence
merchant
militia
musket
rebel
strategy
tariff

Clues

Down

1. army of volunteer citizens
2. to fight against laws
3. plan
4. person who sells goods for profit

Across

5. tax
6. gun with long barrel
7. ruling or governing oneself
8. partner or supporter

Name ____________________

Assessment

Draw a line to match the words and definitions.

rebel	**colonist loyal to British rule**
colony	**essay about current events or ideas**
independence	**fight against**
pamphlet	**soldiers who fought at a minute's notice**
Patriot	**ruling oneself**
Loyalist	**land ruled by faraway country**
Minutemen	**colonist who wanted freedom from British rule**

Overview The United States Constitution

Directions and Sample Answers for Activity Pages

Day 1	See "Provide a Real-World Example" below.
Day 2	Read aloud the title and directions. Read aloud the passage with students. Guide them to fill in the missing words using the words in the word box. (federal, Articles of Confederation, union, states, federal, Congress)
Day 3	Read aloud the title and directions. Read aloud the sentences with students. Guide them to circle the word that correctly completes each sentence. (amend, delegates, Bill of Rights, executive, checks and balances, Congress, House of Representatives, republic, judicial, Supreme Court)
Day 4	Read aloud the title and directions. Help students read the clues and find answers in the word box. Model how to write a word into the crossword puzzle.
Day 5	Read aloud the directions. Allow time for students to complete the tasks. Afterward, meet individually with students to discuss their results. Use their responses to plan further instruction and review.

Provide a Real-World Example

- **Ask:** *What are some laws in our state? What are some laws in our country? Who came up with these laws? Why do we have laws?* (Allow responses.) *Laws, such as wearing your seat belt, are made to protect people. Representatives in state and national government come up with the laws. Because our government is a democracy, citizens vote for the representatives who work in state and national government and make the laws. Citizens make sure that governments work to protect their rights and freedoms.* Write **representative**, **state**, **national**, **government**, **democracy**, **rights**, and **freedom** on chart paper or the board.
- **Ask:** *What was the name of the very first set of laws for the nation?* (Allow responses.) Then **say:** *The Constitution of the United States was the very first set of laws written for the country. It was signed on September 17, 1787.* Write **constitution** on the chart paper.
- Hand out the Day 1 activity page. Read aloud the title and directions. **Say:** *I know the president is the head of the executive branch. Let's write **president** under "Executive." Congress makes the laws for our nation, so let's write it under "Legislative."* Continue to guide students as needed, or allow them to work independently.

Name ____________________

Three Branches of Government

Write each word in the word box under the correct branch of government.

cabinet	**Capitol**	**Congress**	**House of Representatives**	
president	**Senate**	**Supreme Court**	**vice president**	**White House**

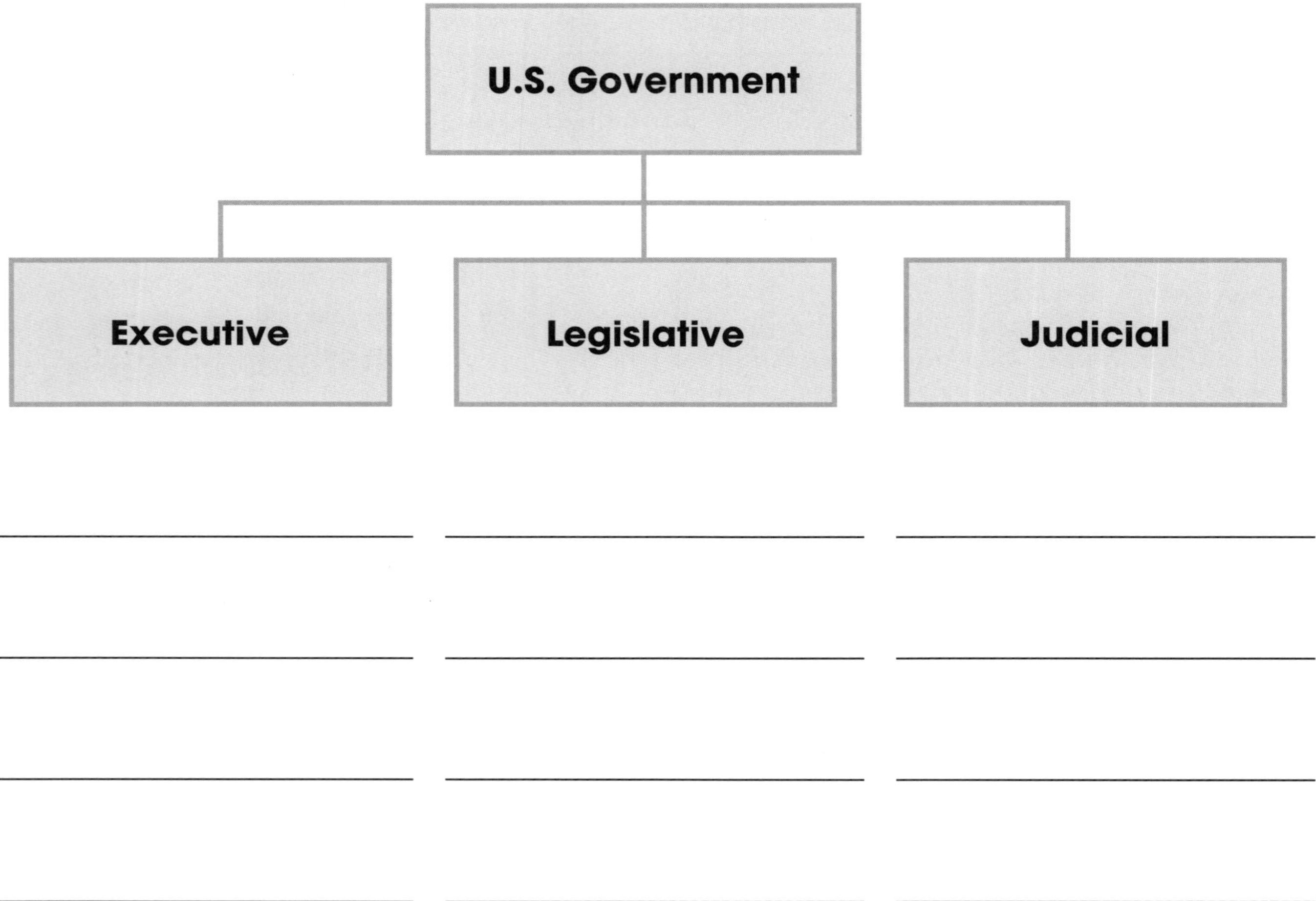

Continental Congress

Read the passage. Write the word from the word box that best completes each sentence. You may use a word more than once.

Articles of Confederation	Congress	federal	states	union

The original thirteen colonies did not want a strong ______________________, or central, government. Each colony wanted to make its own decisions. A document called the ______________________ was written based on those ideas. The Articles set up a loose ______________________ of independent colonies, or ______________________. The states had more power than the ______________________ government. The central law-making branch of the government was called ______________________.

Name ________________________________

Circle It!

Read the sentences. Draw a circle around the word that best completes each sentence.

Americans decided to **amend/appoint**, or change, the Constitution by adding ten important sentences.

Alexander Hamilton invited **democrats/delegates** from each state to a meeting to make decisions about the new government.

The **Bill of Rights/Constitutional Convention** contains the first ten amendments to the Constitution.

The **legislative/executive** branch makes sure the laws are followed.

Each branch of government **ratifies/checks and balances** the others.

Congress/The Constitution is made up of the Senate and the **White House/House of Representatives**.

A **Cabinet/republic** is a form of government in which people have the power to make decisions.

The **judicial/executive** branch of the national government is made up of nine justices who meet in the **Capitol Building/Supreme Court**.

Name ______________________________

Crossword Puzzle

Look at the clues. Find the words in the word box. Write the answers in the crossword puzzle.

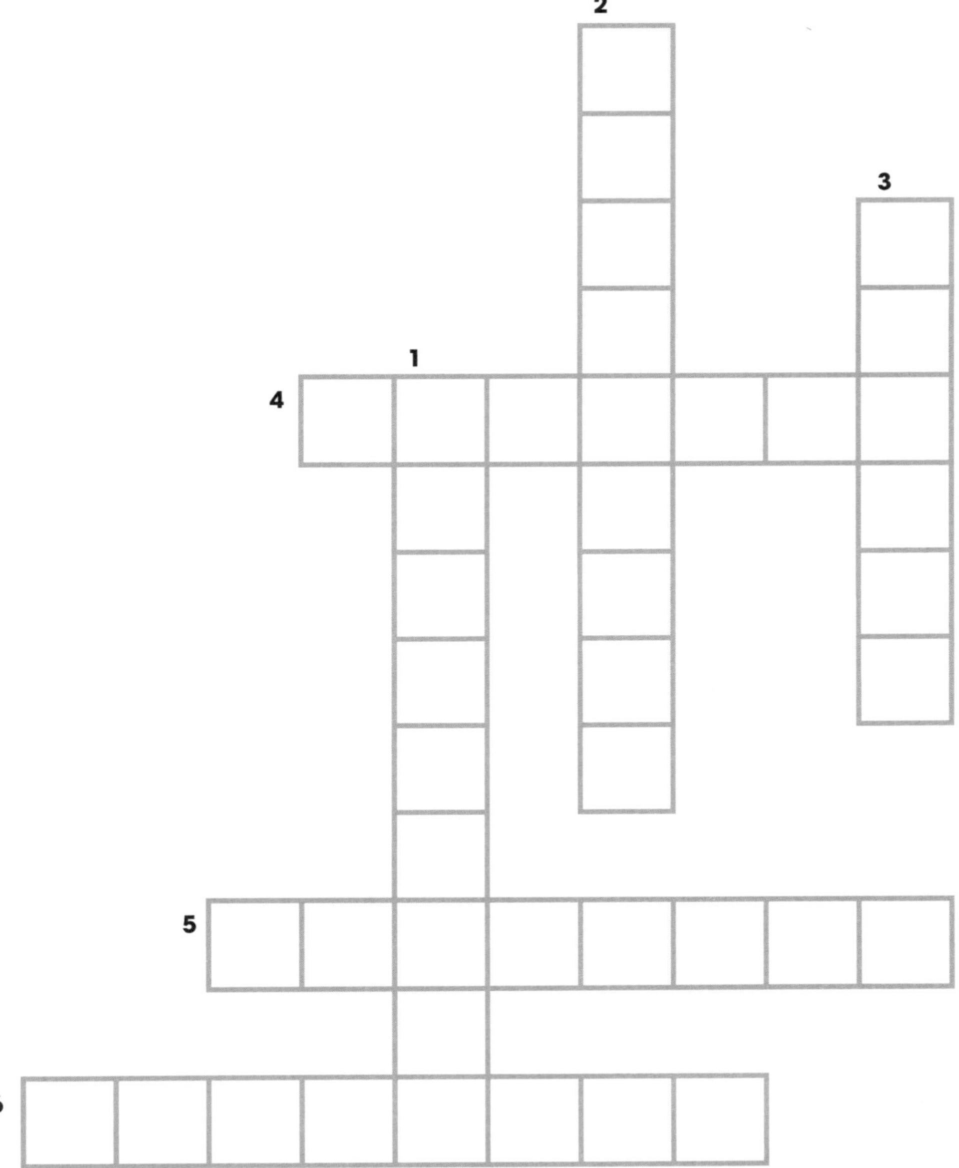

amendment
Cabinet
preamble
president
ratify
senators

Clues

Down

1. formal change
2. head of the executive branch
3. approve a law

Across

4. president's advisers
5. introduction
6. each state has two of them

Assessment

Draw a line to match the words and definitions.

amend	**advisers**
ratify	**change**
Cabinet	**lawmaking body of government**
Congress	**makes sure laws are fair**
judicial branch	**representative**
delegate	**approve a law**

What are some rights that United States citizens have?

____

____

____

____

Overview The Civil War

Directions and Sample Answers for Activity Pages

Day 1	See "Provide a Real-World Example" below.
Day 2	Read aloud the title and directions. Read aloud the passage with students. Guide them to fill in the missing words using the words in the word box. (slavery, territories, secede, states, Confederacy)
Day 3	Read aloud the title and directions. Read aloud the sentences with students. Guide them to circle the word or words that correctly complete each sentence. (Union, advantage, disadvantages, battle, Underground Railroad, amputate, emancipate, Amendment)
Day 4	Read aloud the title and directions. Help students read the clues and find answers in the word box. Model how to write a word into the crossword puzzle.
Day 5	Read aloud the directions. Allow time for students to complete the task. Afterward, meet individually with students to discuss their results. Use their responses to plan further instruction and review.

Provide a Real-World Example

- **Say:** *When you think of war, you probably picture two countries fighting. But that is not always the case. When two regions in the same country are at war, it's called a civil war. Between 1861 and 1865, Americans fought a civil war that split the nation in two and changed it forever. What was the Civil War about? Who were the two sides?* (Allow responses.) *The Civil War was a conflict between the Northern states and the Southern states. There were many causes for the Civil War, but the main issue was slavery.* Write **region**, **Civil War**, **conflict**, and **slavery** on chart paper or the board.
- **Ask:** *Who was in favor of slavery? Who was against it?* (Allow responses.) *The South had a rural way of life and an agricultural economy that depended on slave labor. In contrast, the North's economy was based on trade and industry. Its urban communities were growing. Northerners were against slavery. Abolitionists called for slavery to be outlawed.* Write **rural**, **agricultural**, **economy**, **slave**, **trade**, **industry**, **urban**, and **abolitionist** on the chart paper.
- Hand out the Day 1 activity page. Read aloud the title and directions. **Say:** *I know the South had a rural way of life, so let's write **rural** under "South."* Continue to guide students as needed, or allow them to work independently.

Name ______________________

North vs. South

Write each word in the word box under "North" or "South."

abolitionist	agricultural	Confederacy	industrial	rural
secede	slavery	Underground Railroad	Union	urban

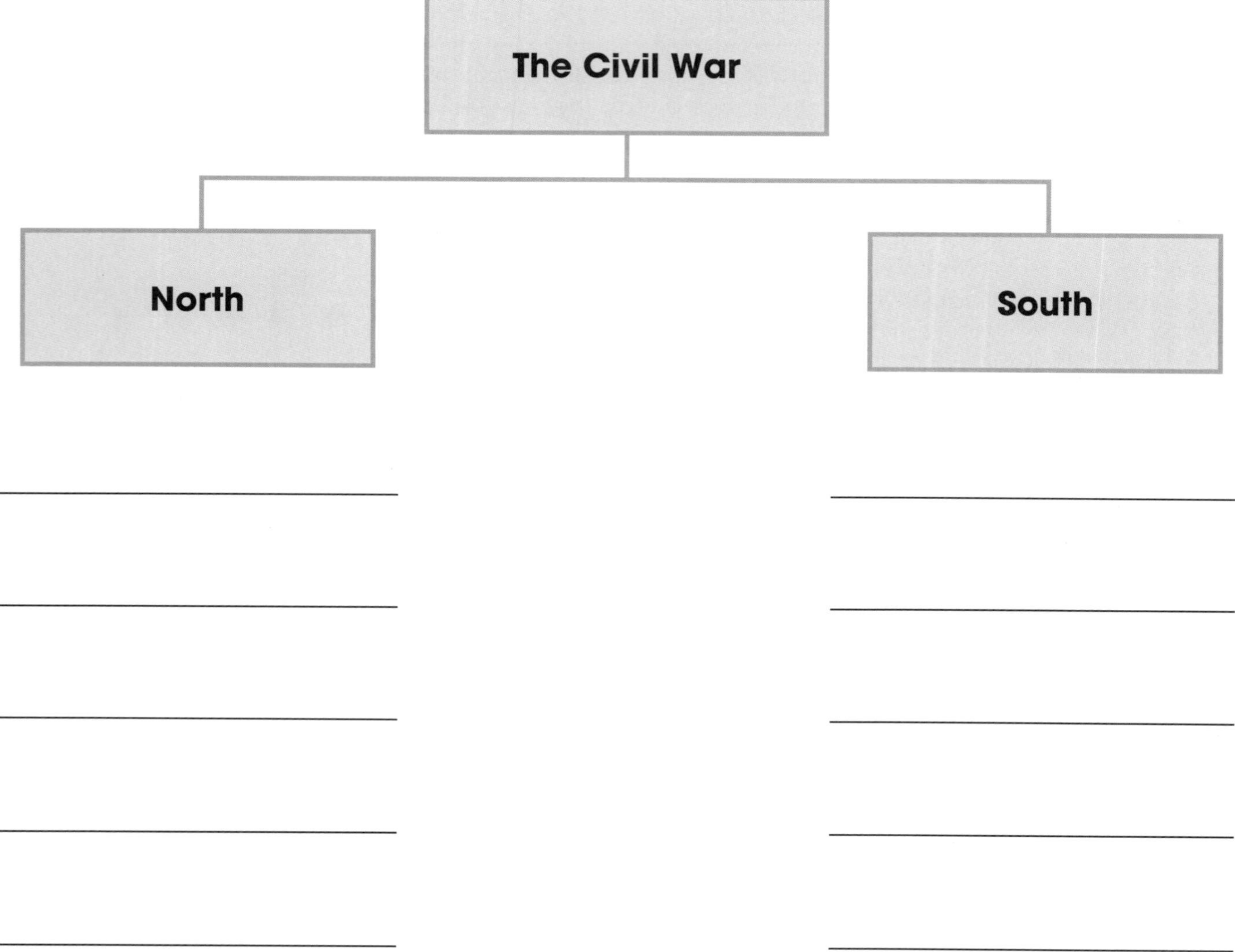

 Name ______________________

The South Secedes

Read the passage. Write the word from the word box that best completes each sentence.

Confederacy	**secede**	**slavery**	**territories**	**states**

During his run for presidency in 1860, Abraham Lincoln promised he would not make laws ending slavery in the South. But he said he did not want ____________________ to spread to the ____________________, or newly settled areas that were not yet states. The South did not believe Lincoln. Southern leaders said that if Lincoln won the election, their states would leave, or ____________________. Lincoln won, and on December 20, 1860, South Carolina seceded. Other Southern ____________________ soon followed. They united to form a new country called the Confederate States of America, or the ____________________.

Name ____________________

Circle It!

Read the sentences. Draw a circle around the word or words that best complete each sentence.

Lincoln said he'd keep the **Union/Confederacy**, or whole country, together.

The North had the **advantage/disadvantage** of having more railroads, which meant it could ship soldiers and supplies more easily than the South.

One of the South's **advantages/disadvantages** was it had fewer men, which meant fewer soldiers.

The first **secession/battle** between the Confederate and Union armies took place at a creek called Bull Run near Washington, D.C.

The **Underground Railroad/Union** was a network of escape routes from the slave states to the free states and Canada.

During the Civil War, doctors sometimes had to **emancipate/amputate** a limb if a wound could not be healed.

When the war broke out, the abolitionists hoped President Lincoln would **emancipate/amputate** the slaves.

The 13th **Amendment/advantage** to the Constitution ended slavery throughout the nation.

 Name ____________________

Crossword Puzzle

Look at the clues. Find the words in the word box. Write the answers in the crossword puzzle.

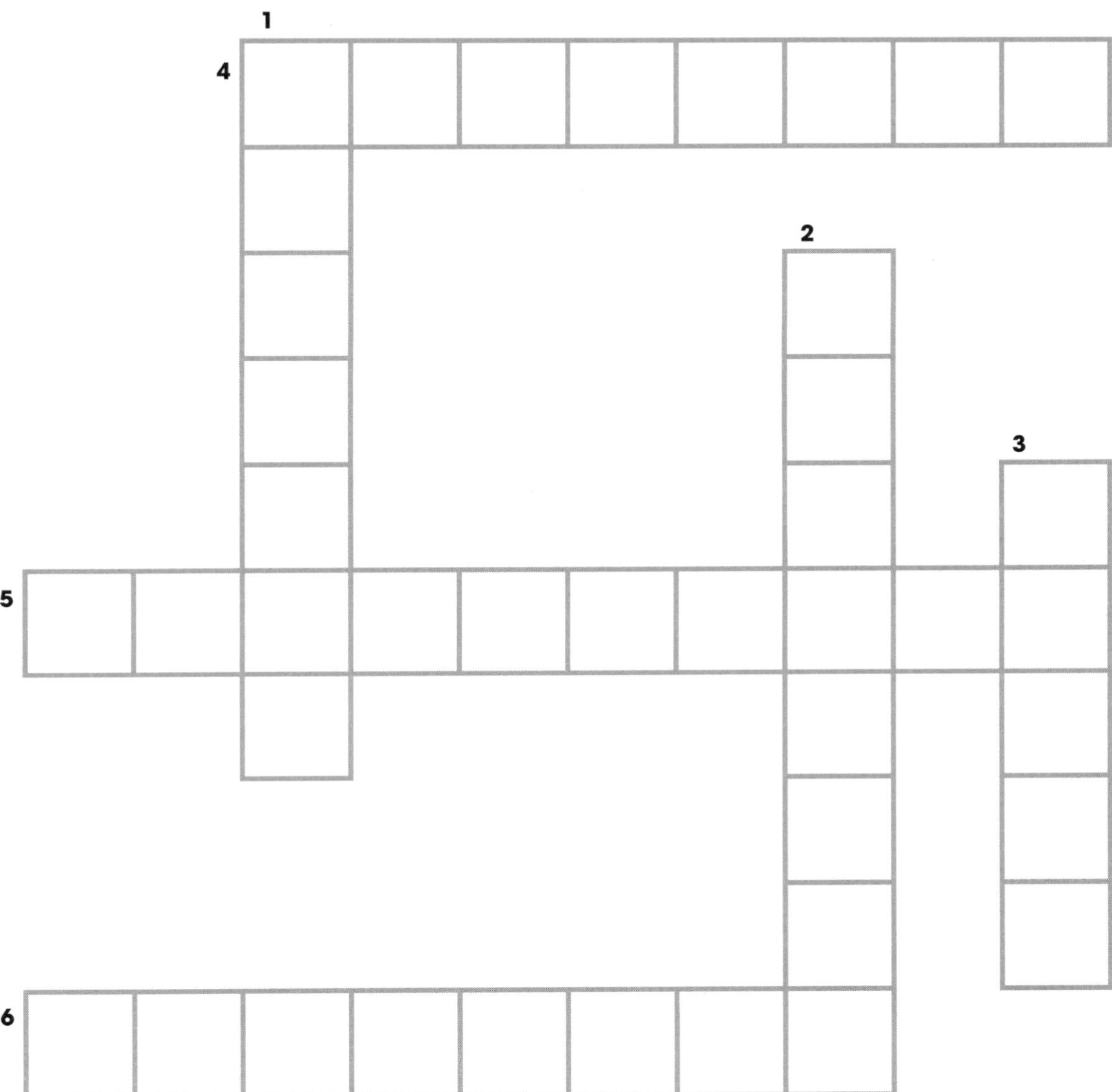

casualty
emancipate
freeman
fugitive
rebel
strategy

Clues

Down

1. one who is not a slave
2. careful plan
3. to fight against one's government

Across

4. person who tries to escape
5. to free from slavery
6. dead or wounded soldier

Name ______________________________

Assessment

Draw a line to match the words and definitions.

emancipate	**person who worked to end slavery**
urban	**withdraw from a union**
Confederacy	**free from slavery**
battle	**remove a limb**
abolitionist	**the practice of owning slaves**
amputate	**a fight between armies**
secede	**city-like**
slavery	**Southern states that seceded from the United States**

Overview Body Systems

Directions and Sample Answers for Activity Pages

Day 1	See "Provide a Real-World Example" below.
Day 2	Read aloud the title and directions. Read aloud the passage with students. Guide them to circle the word that correctly completes each sentence. (cell membrane, cell, cytoplasm, nucleus, genes, organelles, mitochondria)
Day 3	Read aloud the title and directions. Read aloud the passage with students. Guide them to fill in the missing words using the words in the word box. (circulatory, blood, lungs, arteries, capillaries, veins, heart)
Day 4	Read aloud the title and directions. Help students read the clues and find answers in the word box. Model how to write a word into the crossword puzzle.
Day 5	Read aloud the directions. Allow time for students to complete the task. Afterward, meet individually with students to discuss their results. Use their responses to plan further instruction and review.

Provide a Real-World Example

- Put a flower on display. Invite a volunteer to smell the flower. Ask the student to share with the class how the flower smells. Then **say:** *Why are we able to smell things, like a flower?* (Allow responses.) Then have students think about the activities they do every day, like studying, playing sports, etc. **Ask:** *Why are you able to run, jump, ride a bike, think, and learn?* (Allow responses.)

- **Say:** *Your body, and all living things, including plants and animals, have one thing in common that allows you to do the things you do. What do you think it is?* (Allow responses.) *All living things are made of cells. Cells are the building blocks of our bodies. They help us grow, stay healthy, and do the things we do every day.* Write **cells** on chart paper or the board. **Say:** *This week we'll review words we use when describing different body systems, such as **nervous**, **skeletal**, **muscular**, **respiratory**, **circulatory**, and **digestive systems**.* Write these words on the chart paper.

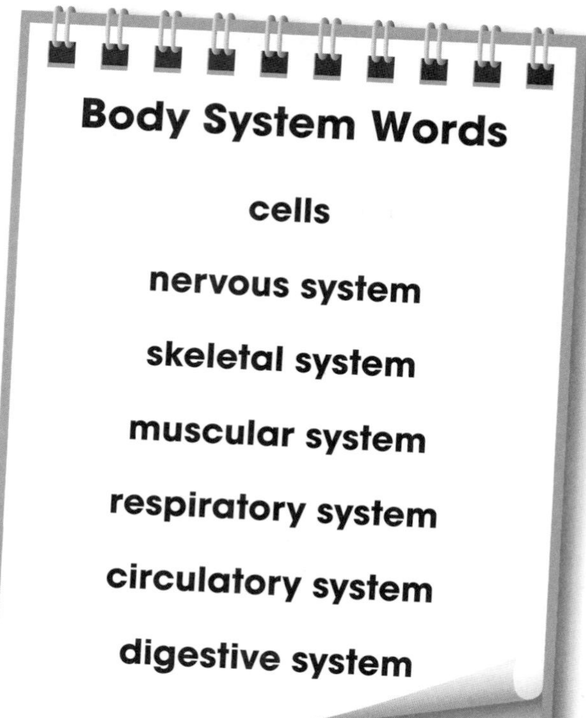

- Hand out the Day 1 activity page. Read aloud the title and directions. **Say:** *I know that the respiratory system has to do with breathing. When I breathe, air flows into my lungs. So lungs must be part of the respiratory system. Let's write **lungs** under "respiratory." Tendons connect muscle to bone. They are part of the muscular system. Let's write **tendons** under "muscular."* Continue to guide students as needed, or allow them to work independently.

Name ______________________

Body Systems

Write each word in the word box under one of the body systems.

blood vessels	**brain**	**cranium**	**diaphragm**	**esophagus**	**lungs**
plasma	**senses**	**small intestine**	**tendons**	**trachea**	**vertebrae**

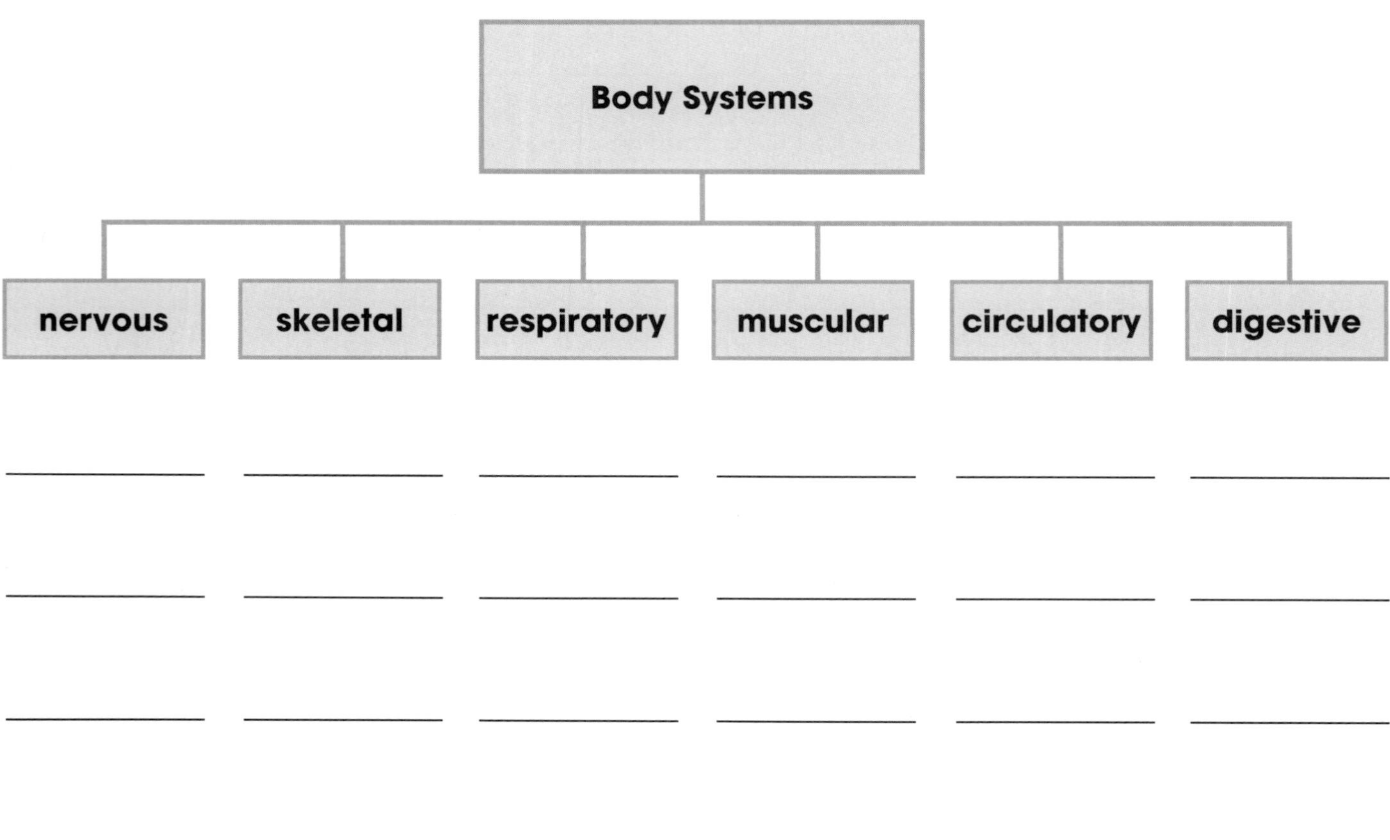

Name ______________________________

Cell Parts

Read the passage. Draw a circle around the correct word in each sentence.

Cells are about 60% water and 40% special parts and chemicals. What keeps everything from leaking out of a cell? The **cell membrane/cytoplasm** is like a bag because it holds all the liquid, chemicals, and other parts of the **chromosome/cell** in one place. It also protects the cell. The watery, jelly-like stuff that contains all the cell parts is the **cytoplasm/nucleus**. The **nucleus/mitochondria** is the cell's control center, telling the cell what to do. The nucleus is controlled by **genes/glucose**, substances that make up part of the body's chemical code. Cells have other parts, or **organelles/organs**, that do special tasks to make the cells work. The **vacuoles/mitochondria**, for example, transform food and nutrients and make energy for cell function.

 Name ____________________

'Round and 'Round Goes the Blood

Read the passage. Write the word from the word box that best completes each sentence. You may use a word more than once.

arteries	blood	capillaries	circulatory
heart	lungs	veins	

Your ______________ system begins at your heart. Your heart pumps oxygen-rich ______________ from your ______________ into your arteries. The ______________ then carry the blood into the major parts of your body, including your brain, liver, and kidneys. Next, tiny ______________ bring the blood to even the smallest parts of your body, such as the air sacs in your lungs, and trade it for oxygen-poor blood. Your ______________ return the blood to your ______________, which pumps it back to your lungs.

 Name ______________________

Crossword Puzzle

Look at the clues. Find the words in the word box. Write the answers in the crossword puzzle.

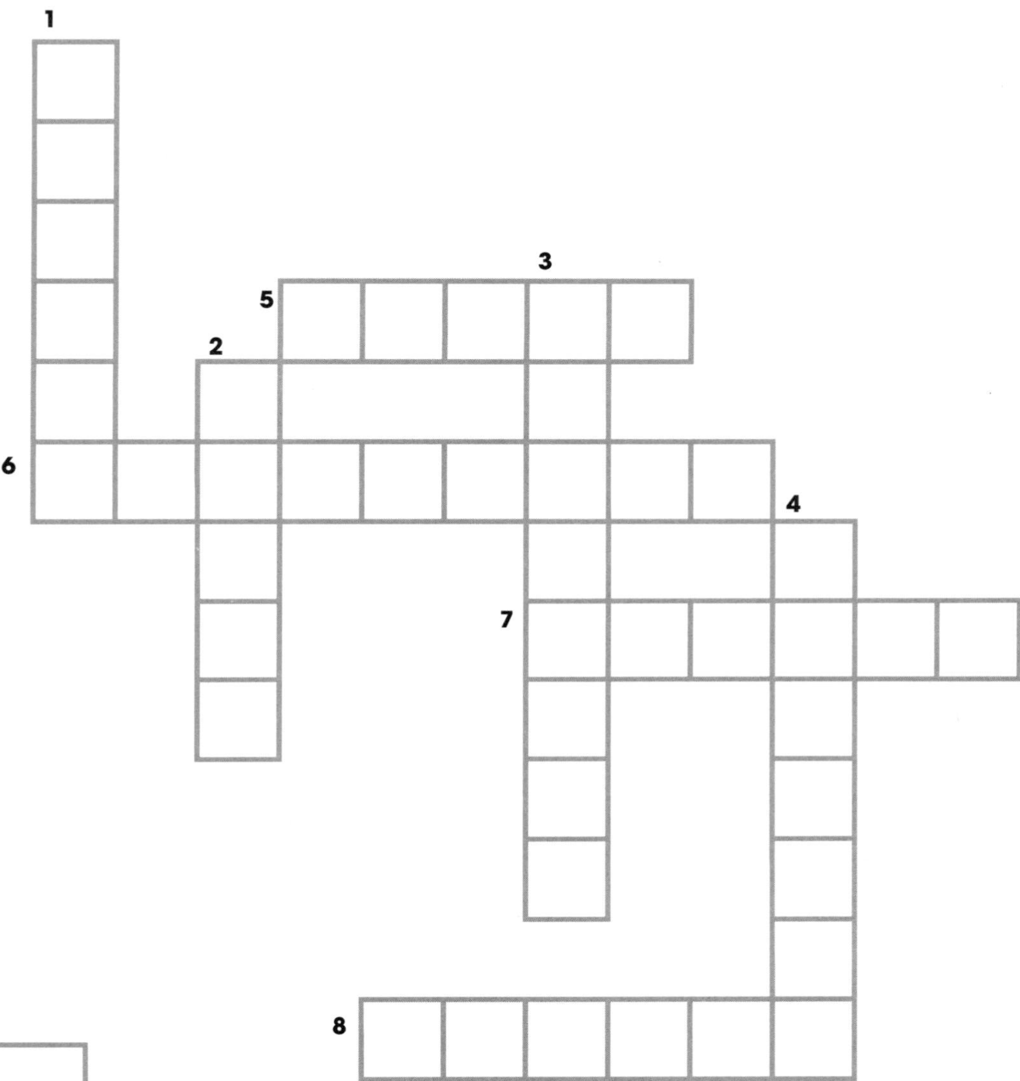

esophagus
joint
ligament
marrow
plasma
skull
tongue
trachea

Clues

Down

1. it has taste buds
2. lets you bend your arms and legs
3. it attaches bones to other bones
4. oxygen travels down it into your lungs

Across

5. protects the brain
6. food travels down it to your stomach
7. helps make red blood cells
8. liquid part of blood

Name ______________________________

Assessment

Draw a line to match the words and definitions.

cell	**tiny blood vessel**
small intestine	**place where bones meet**
veins	**cell's control center**
nucleus	**part of your digestive system**
vertebrae	**carry oxygen-poor blood back to the heart**
capillary	**bones that make up your spine**
lungs	**basic unit of all living things**
joint	**air flows into them**

Overview Earth Science: Water and Weather

Directions and Sample Answers for Activity Pages

Day 1	See "Provide a Real-World Example" below.
Day 2	Read aloud the title and directions. Read aloud the passage with students. Guide them to fill in the missing words using the words in the word box. (water droplets, condensed, Earth, rain, snow, oceans, evaporates, water vapor)
Day 3	Read aloud the title and directions. Read aloud the sentences with students. Guide them to circle the word that correctly completes each sentence. (blizzard, wind, temperatures, tornado, hurricane, ocean, flood, rivers, evacuate)
Day 4	Read aloud the title and directions. Help students read the clues and find answers in the word box. Model how to write a word into the crossword puzzle.
Day 5	Read aloud the directions. Allow time for students to complete the task. Afterward, meet individually with students to discuss their results. Use their responses to plan further instruction and review.

Provide a Real-World Example

- **Ask:** *What's the weather like today? What do you think the weather is like in Africa? The Arctic?* (Allow responses.) *Temperatures on Earth are not all the same. They range on any given day from below 0 degrees to over 100 degrees Fahrenheit.*
- **Ask:** *Why do you think weather is so different in different places?* (Allow responses.) *Temperatures vary because all parts of Earth do not receive the same amount of heat energy from the sun. Differences in temperature of the air cause differences in weather conditions. The sun's energy warms Earth. The atmosphere, a thick layer of greenhouse gases, absorbs and stores energy. The atmosphere also protects Earth from the sun's harmful radiation.* Write **weather**, **temperature**, **energy**, **atmosphere**, **greenhouse gases**, and **radiation** on chart paper or the board.
- Hand out the Day 1 activity page. Read aloud the title and directions. **Say:** *I know that evaporation happens when the sun warms liquid water. Let's write* ***evaporation*** *as part of the water cycle.* Continue to guide students as needed, or allow them to work independently.

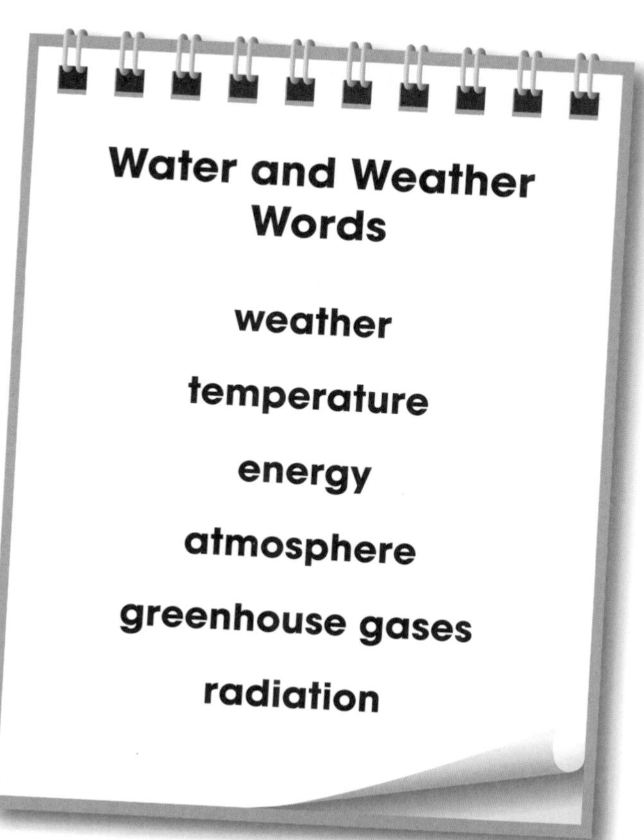

Name ______________________________

The Water Cycle

Fill in the water cycle by writing the words from the word box in the circles in the diagram.

condensation	evaporation	runoff	precipitation

The Water Cycle

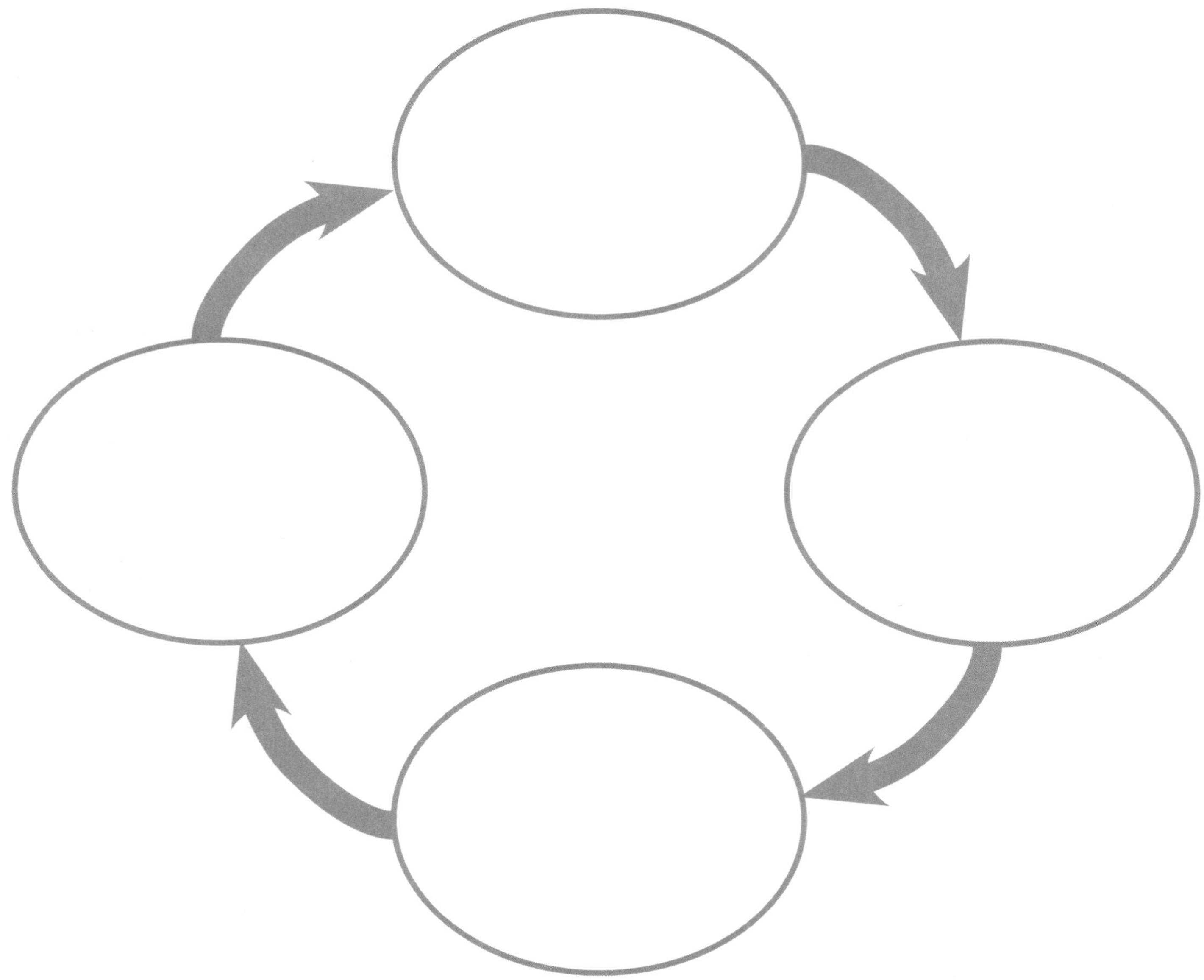

 Name ______________________

Rain Maker

Read the passage. Write the word or words from the word box that best complete each sentence.

condensed	Earth	evaporates	oceans
rain	snow	water droplets	water vapor

Clouds are made up of tiny ______________________ that have ______________________, or changed from gas to liquid. The droplets get bigger and heavier by colliding and combining with other droplets. When the droplets get too heavy, gravity pulls them to ______________________. They come down as ______________________ or, if it's cold, as ______________________. The rain or snow falls into ponds, rivers, lakes, and ______________________. At the same time, water on the ground ______________________ into the air. The gas in the air, or ______________________, forms clouds and the process starts again.

Extreme Weather

Read the passage. Draw a circle around the word that best completes each sentence.

Weather can be extreme sometimes. A **tornado/blizzard** brings a large amount of snow. The **sun/wind** is very strong in a blizzard. A blizzard has very cold **temperatures/thermometers**. A **thunderstorm/tornado** has very strong winds that spin quickly. Tornados move over the ground. A **hurricane/humidity** is a huge storm that brings strong winds and rain. Hurricanes start over the **pond/ocean**. Waves from the ocean bring floods. During a **flood/blizzard**, the large amount of rain causes **air/rivers** to rise. Sometimes people must leave, or **evaporate/evacuate**, their homes to be safe.

Name ____________________

Crossword Puzzle

Look at the clues. Find the words in the word box. Write the answers in the crossword puzzle.

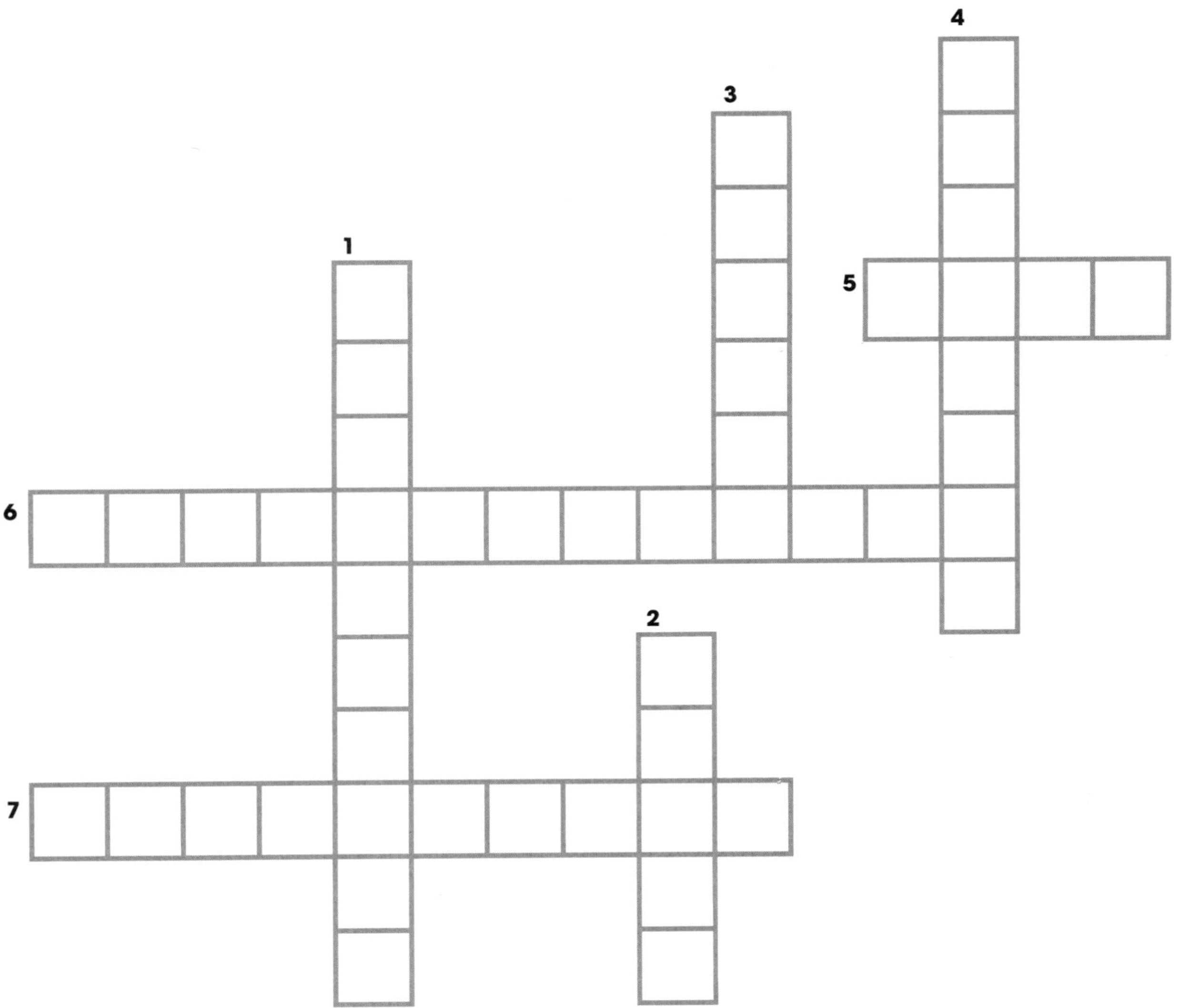

atmosphere
cloud
convection
humidity
meteorologist
spring
wind

Clues

Down

1. layers of air that surround Earth
2. mass of water droplets
3. source of water coming up from the ground
4. amount of moisture in the air

Across

5. air moving over the ground
6. scientist who studies weather
7. movement of heat through liquids and gases

Name ______________________________

Assessment

Draw a line to match the words and definitions.

blizzard	**funnel-shaped storm**
condensation	**measure of hotness or coldness**
evaporation	**sending out of rays of light and heat**
precipitation	**snowstorm**
radiation	**water that is gas in the air**
temperature	**water that falls from the clouds**
tornado	**when water changes to gas**
water vapor	**when water vapor changes to liquid**

Overview Earth Science: Rocks and Minerals

Directions and Sample Answers for Activity Pages

Day 1	See "Provide a Real-World Example" below.
Day 2	Read aloud the title and directions. Read aloud the passage with students. Guide them to fill in the missing words using the words in the word box. (minerals, Earth, elements, diamonds, gemstones, precious metals, gold, ores)
Day 3	Read aloud the title and directions. Read aloud the sentences with students. Guide them to draw a circle around the word or words that correctly complete each sentence. (glacier, sand, mountains, erosion, plates, wind)
Day 4	Read aloud the title and directions. Help students read the clues and find answers in the word box. Model how to write a word into the crossword puzzle.
Day 5	Read aloud the directions. Allow time for students to complete the task. Afterward, meet individually with students to discuss their results. Use their responses to plan further instruction and review.

Provide a Real-World Example

- **Say:** *How old is Earth?* (Allow responses.) *Earth is four and a half million years old! Why do you think geologists study rocks to learn about Earth?* (Allow responses.) Write **Earth**, **geologist**, and **rock** on chart paper or the board.
- **Say:** *Rocks contain clues about what life was like on Earth millions of years ago. Every rock—from a pebble to a boulder—has a story to tell. Sedimentary rock made from layers of sediment—sand, shell, rock, and other small pieces of matter—tells about Earth's past through the fossils it contains. By studying fossils, geologists can learn about living things, including those that are now extinct. Fossils also tell about land and climate changes.* Write **sedimentary**, **sediment**, **sand**, **matter**, and **fossil** on the chart paper.
- Hand out the Day 1 activity page. Read aloud the title and directions. **Say:** *I know that sedimentary rock is made from layers of sediment, such as sand. Let's write **sand** under "Sedimentary." Igneous rock is formed from magma. Let's write **magma** under "Igneous."* Continue to guide students as needed.

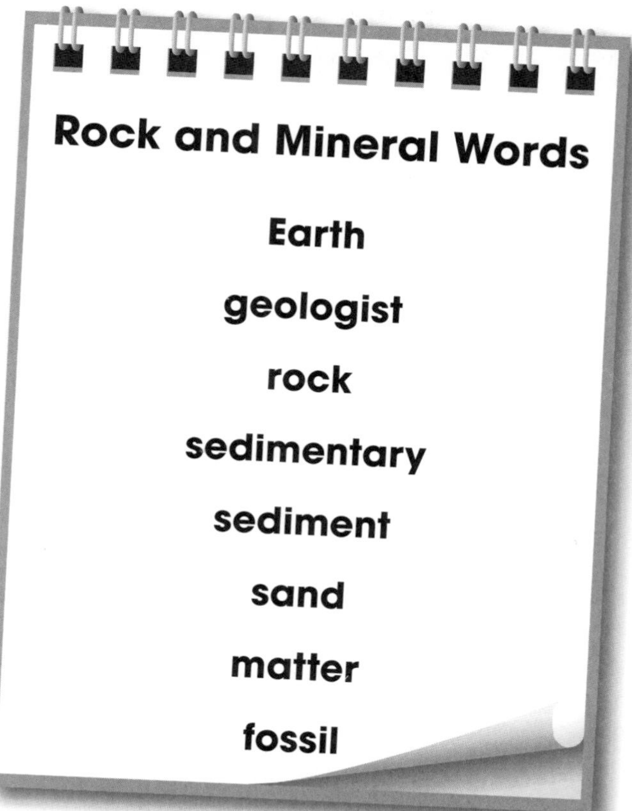

 Name ______________________

Rock On!

Write the words related to each type of rock on the graphic organizer.

lava	magma	marble	molten rock
pressure	sand	sediment	volcano

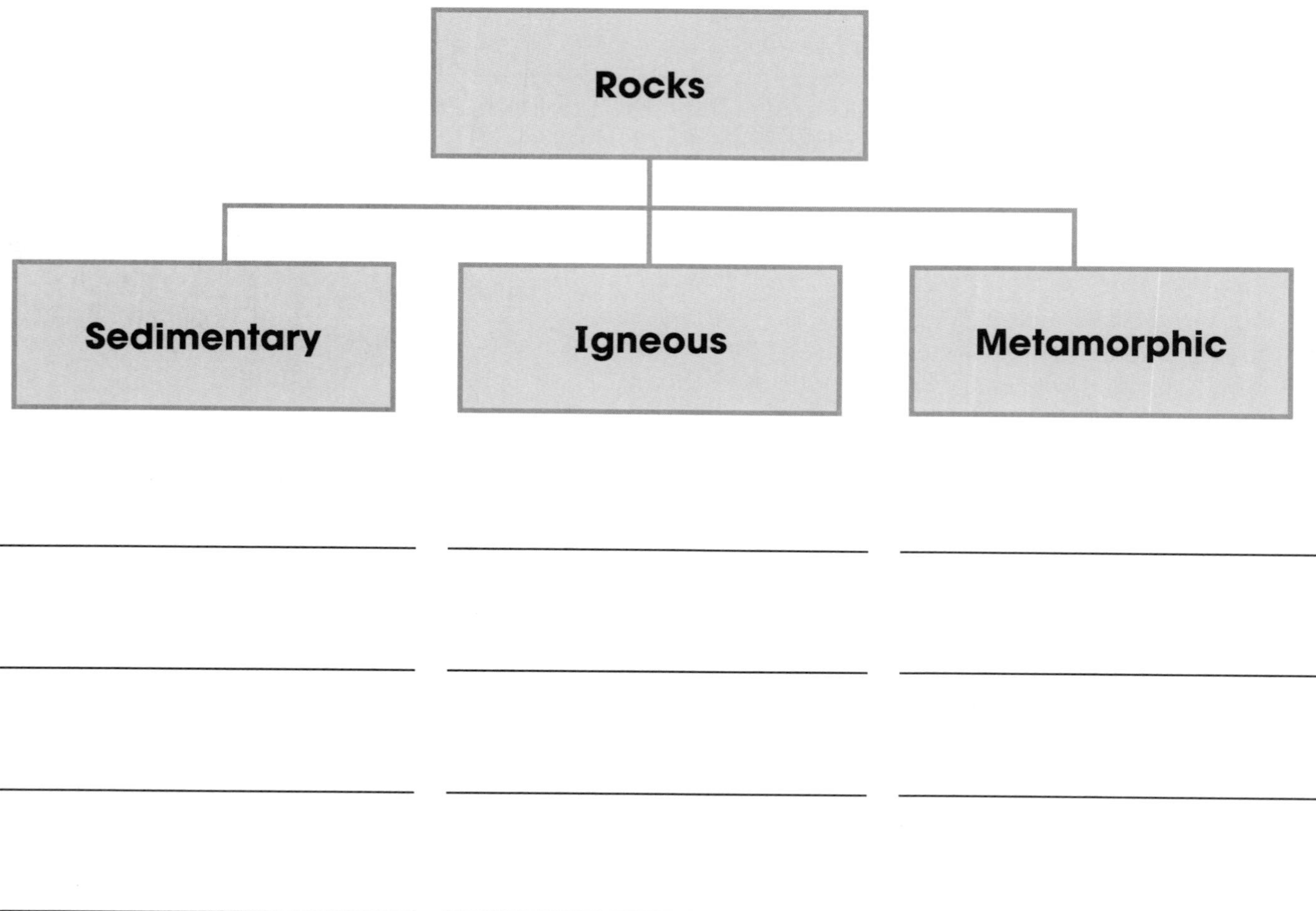

 Name________________________

Minerals

Read the passage. Write the word or words from the word box that best complete each sentence.

diamonds	Earth	elements	gemstones
gold	minerals	ores	precious metals

Rocks are made of ____________________. There are more than 2,000 minerals that naturally occur on ____________________. Minerals are composed of ____________________, the basic building block of all objects on Earth. Gemstones, such as emeralds, rubies, and ____________________, are a rare type of mineral. The hardness of most ____________________ makes them good for jewelry. ____________________, such as copper and ____________________, are found in their pure form in Earth's crust. Rocks that contain useful metals are called ____________________.

Name ______________________________

Circle It!

Read the sentences. Draw a circle around the word or words that best complete each sentence.

When a **landform/glacier** melts, it leaves behind all the rocks and dirt it was carrying.

In some deserts, the wind grinds all the loose rock down into **salt/sand**.

Water cuts canyons through the **mountains/minerals**.

Waves and wind cause constant **earthquakes/erosion** on the beach.

Earth's crust is broken up into giant **precious metals/plates**.

Wind/Water erodes land when there are no trees and plants to keep the earth in place.

Name ____________________

Crossword Puzzle

Look at the clues. Find the words in the word box. Write the answers in the crossword puzzle.

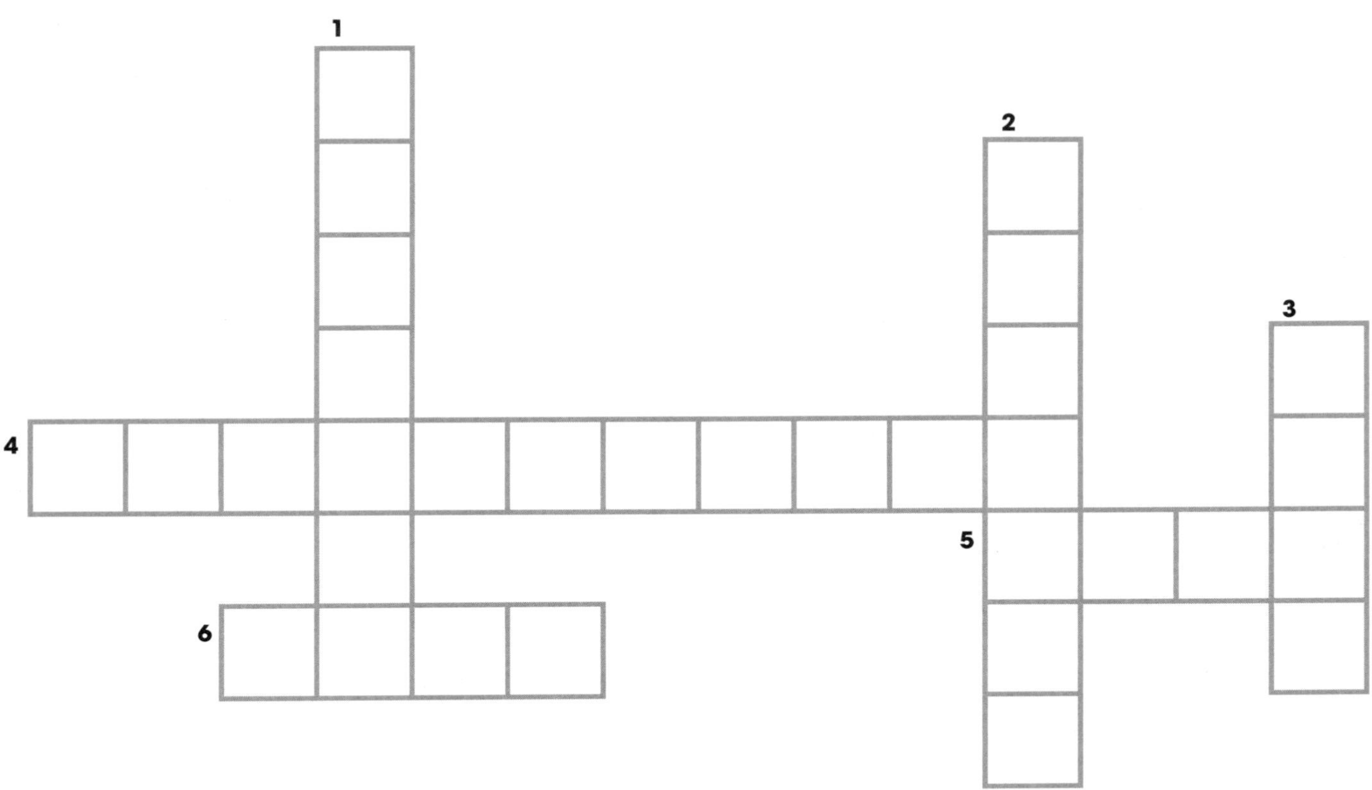

glacier
iron
metamorphic
soil
volcano
wind

Clues

Down

1. opening in Earth's surface
2. piece of ice as big as a mountain
3. moving air that creates sand dunes

Across

4. rock formed from another rock that was changed by pressure or high temperature
5. one of the most common elements on Earth
6. millions of insects make their home in it

Assessment

Draw a line to match the words and definitions.

earthquake	**rock that contains a metal**
erosion	**magma that reaches Earth's surface**
erupt	**section of Earth's crust**
igneous	**burst out with great force**
lava	**rock formed from magma**
mineral	**shaking of Earth's crust**
ore	**solid, natural substance**
plate	**wearing away by wind, water, or ice**

Overview Chemistry

Directions and Sample Answers for Activity Pages

Day 1	See "Provide a Real-World Example" below.
Day 2	Read aloud the title and directions. Read aloud the passage with students. Guide them to fill in the missing words using the words in the word box. (atoms, substance, chemical reaction, reactant, product)
Day 3	Read aloud the title and directions. Read aloud the sentences with students. Guide them to draw a circle around the word or words that correctly complete each sentence. (matter, element, atoms, molecules, particles, chemical change)
Day 4	Read aloud the title and directions. Help students read the clues and find answers in the word box. Model how to write a word into the crossword puzzle.
Day 5	Read aloud the directions. Allow time for students to complete the task. Afterward, meet individually with students to discuss their results. Use their responses to plan further instruction and review.

Provide a Real-World Example

- Prior to the start of this lesson, cut open an apple and place it on display. When the lesson begins, point to the apple and **ask:** *What happened to the white part of the apple? Why?* (Allow responses.) *The white part of the apple turned brown. That's because a chemical change has happened. Chemicals in the apple combined with oxygen in the air. A new type of matter formed.* Write **chemical change**, **chemical**, **oxygen**, and **matter** on chart paper or the board.
- **Ask:** *How have the properties, or characteristics, of the apple changed?* (Allow responses.) Then **say:** *One of the properties that changed is color. It used to be white and now it's brown. Other changed properties are taste and texture.* Write **property** on the chart paper.
- Hand out the Day 1 activity page. Read aloud the title and directions. **Say:** *I know that when an ice cube melts, it looks different but it is still the same kind of matter. When a change makes something look different but it is still the same kind of matter, it's gone through a physical change. When metal, like iron, gets rusty from the air, the matter has changed from iron to rust. Since one matter has changed to another, it is a chemical change. Let's write* ***rusting*** *under "Chemical Changes."* Continue to guide students as needed.

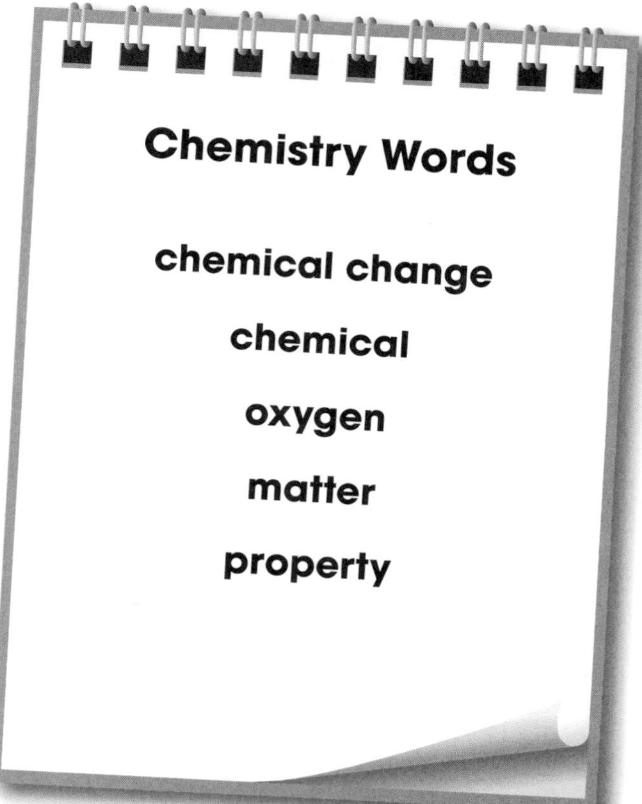

Name ____________________

Physical or Chemical?

Identify each word in the word box as being a physical change or a chemical change.

baking	boiling	cutting
freezing	melting	rusting

Kinds of Changes

Physical Changes	Chemical Changes
____________	____________
____________	____________
____________	____________
____________	____________

Chemical Reactions

Read the passage. Write the word or words from the word box that best complete each sentence.

atoms	chemical reaction	product
reactant	substance	

All matter is made up of ______________________. Sometimes the atoms of one substance interact with the atoms of another ______________________. The atoms rearrange and form something new. This rearrangement of atoms is a ______________________. Each original substance is a ______________________. The new matter that forms is a ______________________.

Circle It!

Read the sentences. Draw a circle around the word or words that best complete each sentence.

Anything that has mass and takes up space is **chemistry/matter**.

An **atom/element** is a pure substance. It does not break down into something else.

Atoms/Molecules are the smallest bits of elements.

Atoms can combine to form **molecules/elements**.

Atoms are the smallest pieces, or **particles/molecules**, of any element.

Iron turning to rust is an example of a **chemical formula/chemical change**.

Name ______________________________

Crossword Puzzle

Look at the clues. Find the words in the word box. Write the answers in the crossword puzzle.

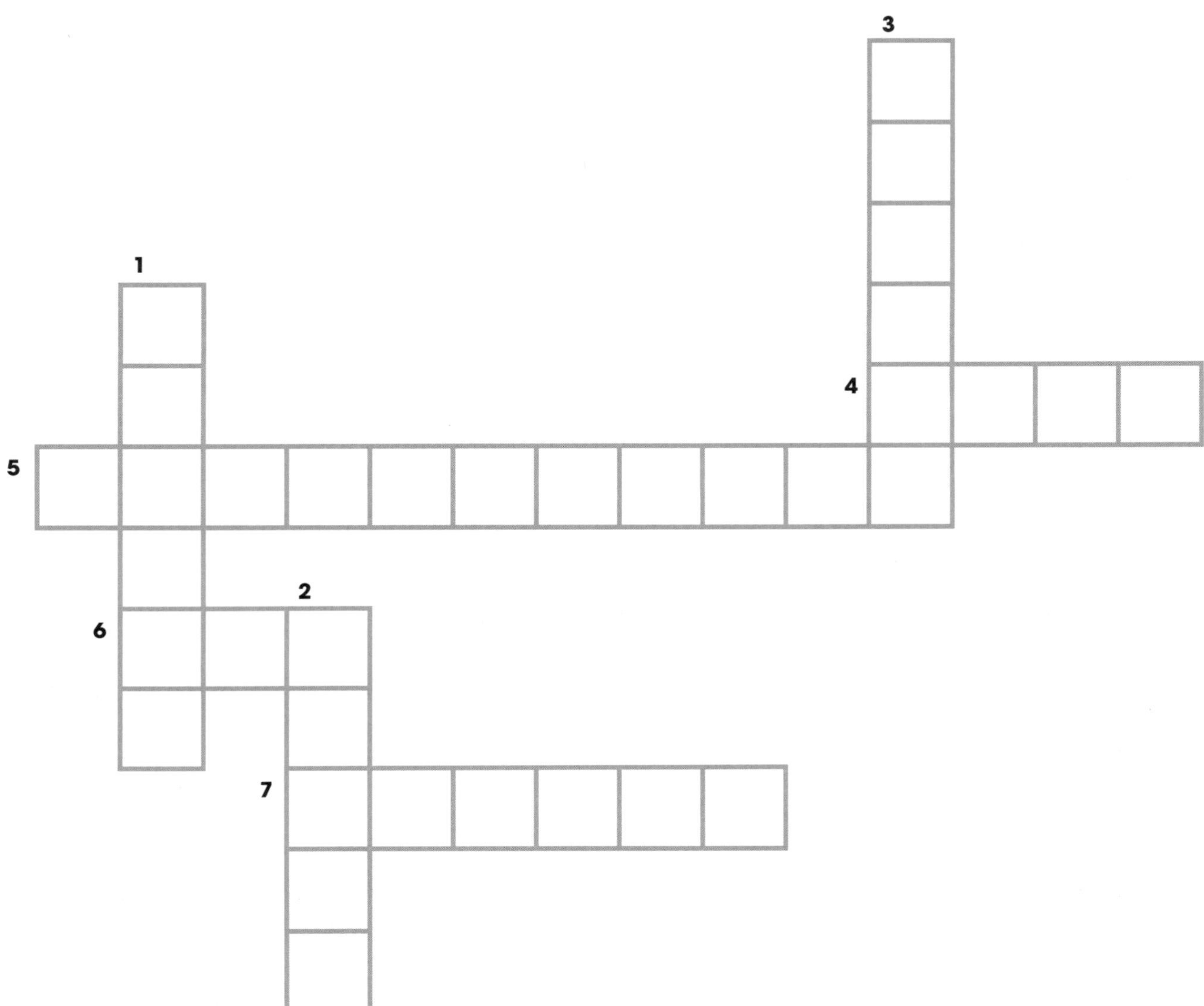

energy
gas
liquid
mass
solid
temperature
volume

Clues

Down

1. produces heat
2. matter that keeps its shape
3. amount of space an object takes up

Across

4. amount of matter in an object
5. measurement of how hot or cold an object is
6. steam
7. water

Name ______________________________

Assessment

Draw a line to match the words and definitions.

atom	**characteristic**
molecule	**basic kind of matter found in nature**
oxygen	**tiny building block of matter**
element	**smallest piece that makes up an element**
property	**chopping and slicing**
physical changes	**it causes chemical changes**

Overview Fractions and Decimals

Directions and Sample Answers for Activity Pages

Day 1	See "Provide a Real-World Example" below.
Day 2	Read aloud the title and directions. Help students make a match between the items in the left column and the words in the right column.
Day 3	Read aloud the title and directions. Help students identify the missing word in each sentence and write it on the line.
Day 4	Read aloud the title and directions. Help students draw a circle around the symbol that correctly compares the numbers.
Day 5	Read aloud the directions. Allow time for students to complete the tasks. Afterward, meet individually with students to discuss their results. Use their responses to plan further instruction and review.

Provide a Real-World Example

- Write the fraction ½ on chart paper or the board. **Ask:** *How do you show the fraction ½ as a decimal?* (Allow responses.) Write the answer on the board, and model how to find the decimal equivalent by dividing the numerator by the denominator. Point out how to add a decimal point and zeros to the dividend: 1 = 1.0. Write **fraction**, **decimal**, **decimal point**, and **dividend** on chart paper.
- Now **say:** *Baseball fans follow players' statistics by using decimal equivalents to figure out batting averages. They divide the number of hits by the number of times a player has been at bat.*
- Hand out the Day 1 activity page. Read aloud the title and directions. Model answers as needed.

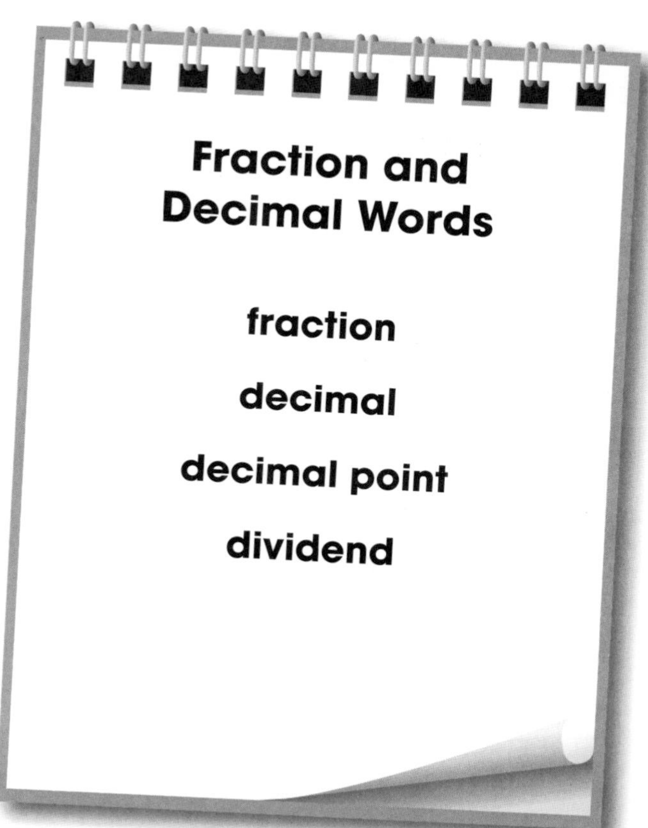

Name ______________________________

Baseball Stats

Draw a circle around the correct answer.

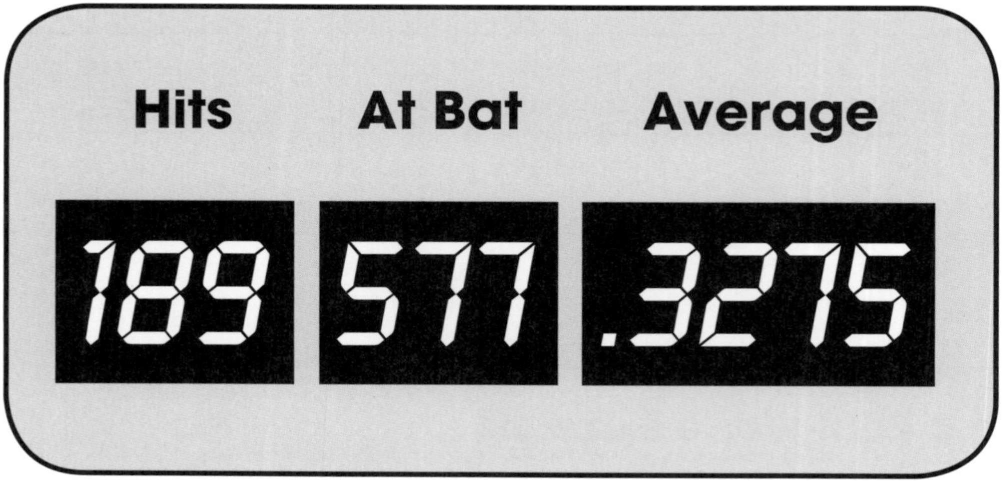

Which number is in the tenths place in Smith's average? **3** **2** **7**

Which is the thousandths place in Smith's average? **3** **2** **7**

Which shows Smith's average rounded to the nearest hundredth? **.33** **.328** **.3**

 Name ____________________

Match-Up!

Draw a line to make a match.

$\frac{2}{5}$ and $\frac{4}{10}$	**denominator**
$3\frac{3}{5}$	**equivalent decimals**
0.06④	**equivalent fractions**
0.14 and 0.140	**equal parts**
17	**thousandths place**
$\frac{⑤}{16}$	**mixed number**
$\frac{3}{⑤}$	**whole number**
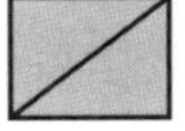	**numerator**

Name ______________________________

Money, Money, Money

Complete each sentence using the words in the word boxes.

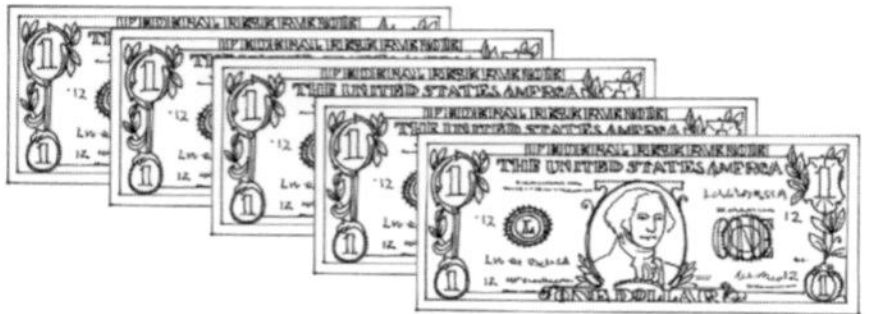

=

ones		tenths	hundredths
5	.	6	8

We have ______________________ ones.

We have ______________________ tenths.

We have ______________________ hundredths.

eight
five
six

=

ones		tenths	hundredths
10	.	4	2

We have ten ______________________.

We have four ______________________.

We have two ______________________.

hundredths
ones
tenths

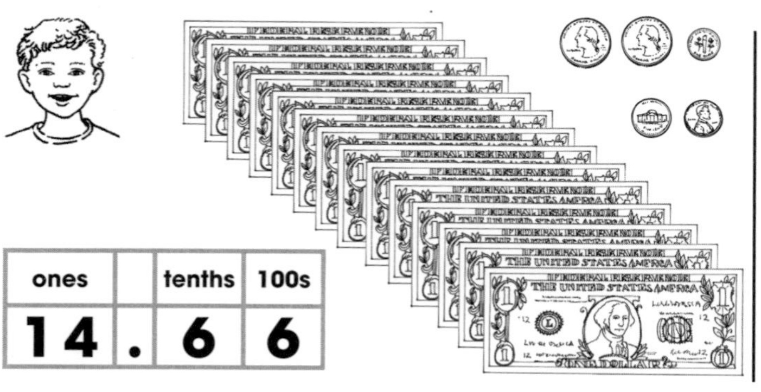

ones		tenths	100s
14	.	6	6

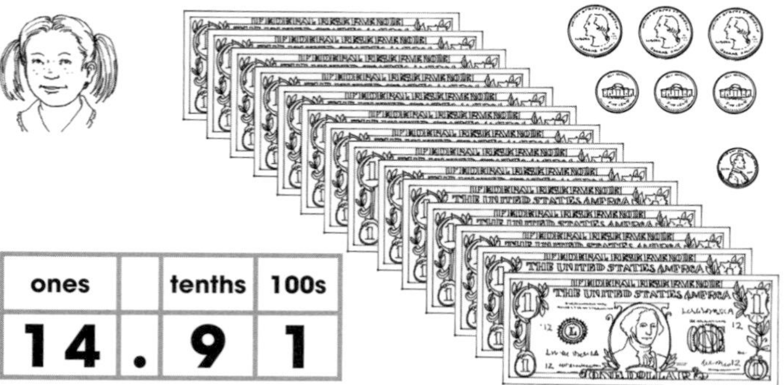

ones		tenths	100s
14	.	9	1

boy	girl	hundredths	ones	tenths

The girl has more in the ______________________ place than the boy.

The boy has more in the ______________________ place than the girl.

The boy and girl have equivalent amounts in the ______________________ place.

The ______________________ has more money than the ______________________.

 Name ______________________________

Comparing Decimals

Draw a circle around the symbol that correctly completes each sentence.

0.50 is | < | > | = | 0.25.

0.50 is | < | > | = | 0.75.

0.50 is | < | > | = | 0.5.

Seventy-hundredths is   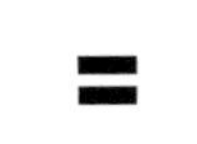 seven-tenths.

One-tenth is   | = | one.

Eighty-five hundredths is  | > | = | seven-tenths.

Name ______________________________

Assessment

Draw a circle around the answers.

In the fraction $\frac{6}{15}$, which number is the denominator? **15** **6** **1**

In the mixed number $1\frac{3}{5}$, which number is the numerator? **1** **3** **5**

In the mixed number $3\frac{5}{8}$, which number is the whole number? **8** **5** **3**

Which fraction is equivalent to $\frac{2}{5}$? $\frac{6}{15}$ $\frac{5}{2}$ $\frac{2}{10}$

Which decimal is equivalent to 0.23? **0.230** **0.023** **2.30**

Which means the same as 0.38?

thirty-eight hundredths **thirty-eight tenths** **thirty-eight**

Which number is in the thousandths place in 3.791? **3** **1** **9**

Shade three-eighths of the pizza pie.

Overview Multiplication

Directions and Sample Answers for Activity Pages

Day 1	See "Provide a Real-World Example" below.
Day 2	Read aloud the title and directions. Remind students that place value is the value of a digit in a number based on its location. Help students identify the written numbers.
Day 3	Read aloud the title and directions. Help students identify the missing word or words in each sentence and write the word or words on the line.
Day 4	Read aloud the title and directions. Remind students that a multiple of a number is any number that is a product of the number. Help students identify the multiples of seven in order. Guide them to draw a line from one multiple of seven to the next through the maze.
Day 5	Read aloud the directions. Allow time for students to complete the tasks. Afterward, meet individually with students to discuss their results. Use their responses to plan further instruction and review.

Provide a Real-World Example

- **Say:** *Imagine your friend is running in a marathon. You want to estimate, or make a rough guess, about how long the race will take her to run. A marathon is 26.2 miles. Your friend runs a mile in ten minutes. How can you figure out how long the race will take?* (Allow responses.) Write **estimate** on chart paper or the board. **Say:** *To figure out how long the race will take to run, multiply the distance (26.2) by her pace (ten minutes per mile).* Write **multiply** on the chart paper. Then **say:** *This would take time to calculate, so instead, we can use estimation to figure out about how long it will take her to run the race. To estimate, first we round the numbers so they are easier to work with. We can round to the nearest tens. In the decimal number 26.2, the number to the right of the decimal, in the tenths place, is 2, so round down to 26. 26 multiplied by 10 is 260. We can estimate that the race will take her 260 minutes to run. An estimate is not exact, but it gives us a reasonable answer.* Write **estimation**, **round**, **decimal**, **tenths**, and **reasonable answer** on the chart paper.

- Hand out the Day 1 activity page. Read aloud the title and directions. **Say:** *To quickly figure out the sum of two big numbers, we estimate by rounding numbers. Write* ***estimate*** *on the first line and* ***round*** *on the second line.* Continue to guide students as needed.

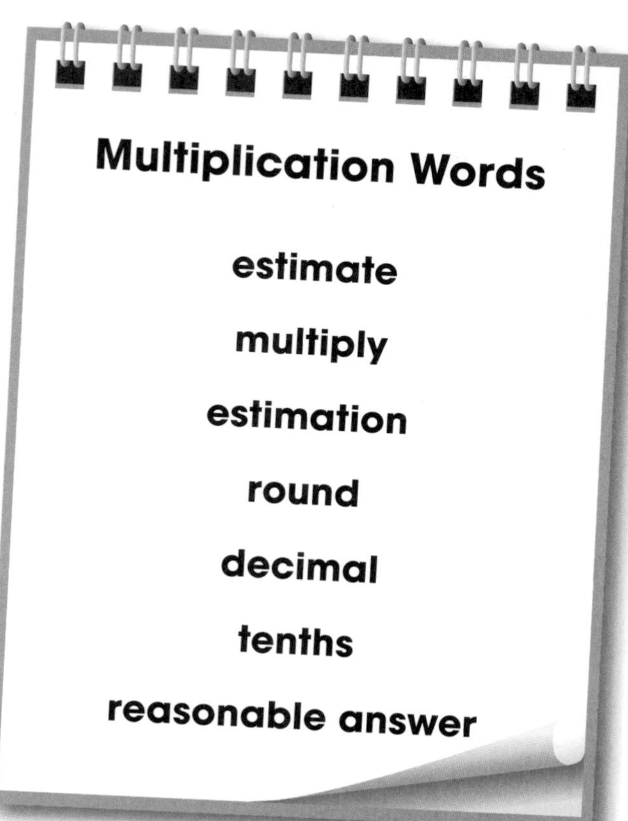

Name ____________________

Cloze It Up!

Read the sentences. Use the words in the word box to complete each sentence. Write the words on the lines.

decimal	estimate	hundreds	place
place value	reasonable answer	round	tens

To ____________________ the sum of two numbers, such as 535 + 721, ____________________ each number: 500 + 700. Then add the rounded numbers. The sum won't be exact, but it will be a ____________________.

____________________ is the value of a digit in a number based on the location of the digit. In the number 293, the place value of 2 is ____________________. The ____________________ value of 3 is ones and the place value of 9 is ____________________.

A ____________________ point separates the ones places from the tenths place in decimals.

Name ______________________

A Place for Every Number

Read the place values on the left. Draw a circle around the numeral the words describe.

two tens and three ones	**23**	**32**	**203**
nine tens and seven ones	**970**	**79**	**97**
three hundreds, four tens, and two ones	**432**	**32**	**342**
one hundred, zero tens, and three ones	**103**	**130**	**13**
six hundreds, six tens, and zero ones	**606**	**660**	**60**
zero hundreds, one ten, and nine ones	**19**	**91**	**109**
nine hundreds, three tens, and four ones	**943**	**493**	**934**
five hundreds, five tens, and three ones	**535**	**553**	**355**

Name ______________________

Equal Groups

Complete each sentence by writing the correct word or words.

5	**x**	$\frac{1}{2}$	**=**	$2\frac{1}{2}$
five	multiplied by	one-half	is equal to	two and one-half

We see ______________________ equal groups.

We see ______________________ of a pizza pie in each group.

The product is ______________________.

five
one-half
two and one-half

7	**x**	**1.50**	**=**	**10.50**
seven	multiplied by	one and fifty-hundredths	is equal to	ten and fifty-hundredths

The number seven is a ______________________.

The ______________________ one and five-tenths is also a factor.

The decimal ten and five-tenths is the ______________________.

The number one in the product is in the tens ______________________.

decimal
factor
place
product

9	**x**	$\frac{1}{4}$	**=**	$2\frac{1}{4}$
nine	multiplied by	one-fourth	is equal to	two and one-fourth

Nine multiplied by one-fourth cups ______________________ two and one-fourth cups.

The mixed number two and one-fourth is the ______________________.

The number ______________________ is a factor.

is equal to
nine
product

Multiple Maze

Help Lucky Duck get back to the pond. Make a path following the multiples of 7 in order.

Name ____________________

Assessment

Draw a circle around the answer.

Which is a multiple of nine?	**17**	**81**	**92**
Which number shows sixty-four rounded to the nearest ten?	**60**	**70**	**65**
Which number is in the hundreds place in 814?	**1**	**4**	**8**
In the equation 0.04 x 32 = 1.28, which is a factor?	**1.28**	**0.04**	**=**
In the equation 3 x 4.6 = 13.8, which is the product?	**13.8**	**4.6**	**3**
Which number is 13.8 rounded to the closest one?	**13**	**8**	**14**

What is your age rounded to the nearest ten? Write it on the line.

____

Overview Division

Directions and Sample Answers for Activity Pages

Day 1	See "Provide a Real-World Example" below.
Day 2	Read aloud the title and directions. Help students identify the number that correctly completes each sentence and write it on the line.
Day 3	Read aloud the title and directions. Help students identify the missing word or words in each sentence and write the word or words on the line.
Day 4	Read aloud the title and directions. Help students read the clues and find answers in the word box. Model how to write a word into the crossword puzzle.
Day 5	Read aloud the directions. Allow time for students to complete the task. Afterward, meet individually with students to discuss their results. Use their responses to plan further instruction and review.

Provide a Real-World Example

- **Say:** *Imagine we are having a class party. My receipt for all the food and decorations comes to a total of $180. Now let's say there are 24 students in the class and each student is to pay the same amount, or equal groups. How could I figure it out?* (Allow responses.) *We use division to calculate the answer.*

- Write 180 ÷ 24 on chart paper or the board. Point to each part of the equation as you **say:** *180 is the dividend, or number to be divided. 24 is the divisor, or number we are dividing by. The result, or quotient, will be how much each student owes.* Challenge students to calculate the answer. Then show them how to divide these numbers. **Say:** *180 divided by 24 is equal to seven point five, or seven dollars and fifty cents. This number is a decimal, or a whole number and a fraction.* Write the words **equal groups**, **division**, **dividend**, **divide**, **divisor**, **quotient**, **divided by**, **is equal to**, and **decimal** on the chart paper.

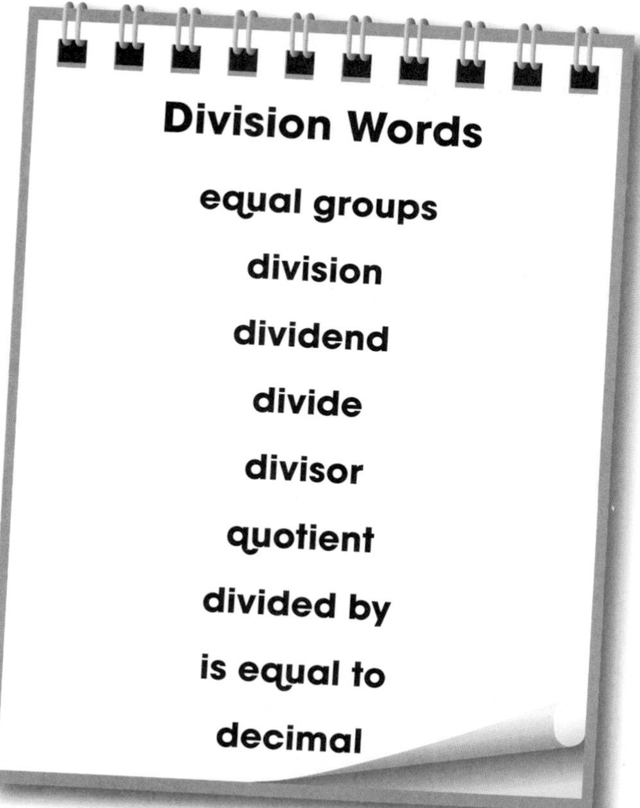

- Hand out the Day 1 activity page. Read aloud the title and directions. Draw attention to the first item on the left side. **Say:** *When you see this symbol in an equation, it means the number to the left of the sign is to be divided by the number to the right. Draw a line to the words* ***divided by***. Focus attention on the next item. **Say:** *The number circled is the quotient, or result of dividing a number.* Continue to guide students as needed.

Name ______________________________

Mathematical Match-Up

Draw a line to match the items in the left column with the words and phrases in the right column.

208 ÷ 52 = 4	**dividend**
25 ÷ 45 = 0.55	**is equal to**
225 ÷ 50 = 4.5	**divided by**
985 ÷ 5 = 197	**decimal**
39 ÷ 90 = .43	**quotient**
464 ÷ 32 = 14.5	**divisor**

Name ______________________________

Equal Groups

Complete each sentence by writing the correct number on the line.

I see ______________________ trees in all.

I see ______________________ rows of trees.

I see ______________________ trees in each row.

I see ______________________ columns of trees.

I see ______________________ trees in each column.

One hundred forty divided by ten is equal to ______________________.

One hundred forty divided by fourteen is equal to ______________________.

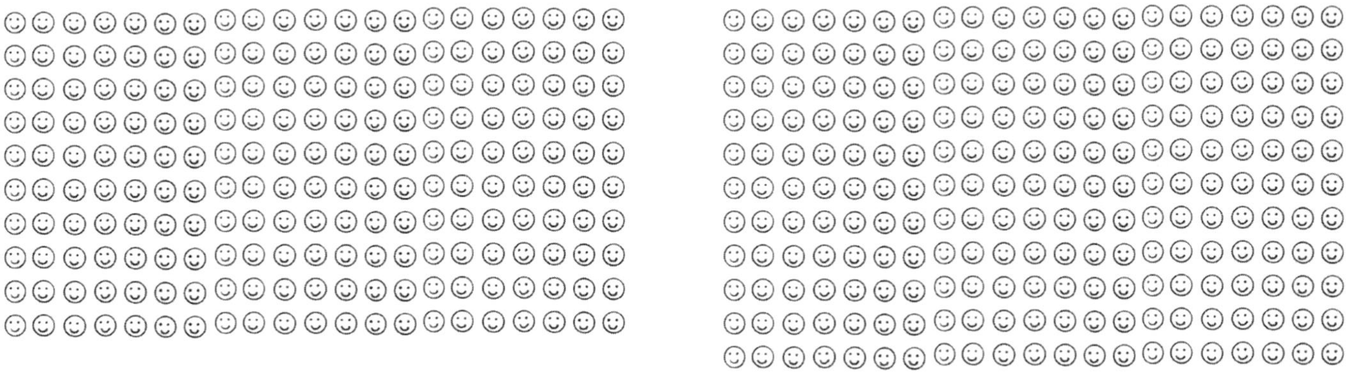

I see ______________________ stickers in all.

I see ______________________ rows of stickers.

I see ______________________ stickers in each row.

I see ______________________ columns of stickers.

I see ______________________ stickers in each column.

Four hundred forty-one divided by twenty-one is equal to ______________________.

 Name ______________________________

Apple Bags

Complete each sentence using the words in the word boxes.

480 ÷ 16 = 30

dividend	divisor	quotient

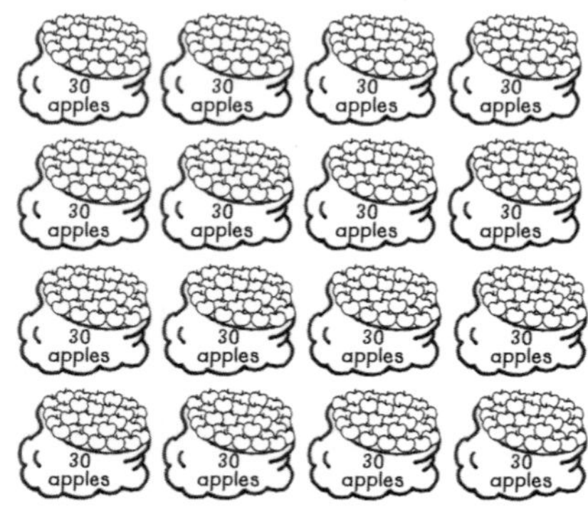

The number 480 is the ____________________.

The number 30 is the ____________________.

The number 16 is the ____________________.

240 ÷ 12 = 20

twelve	twenty	two hundred forty

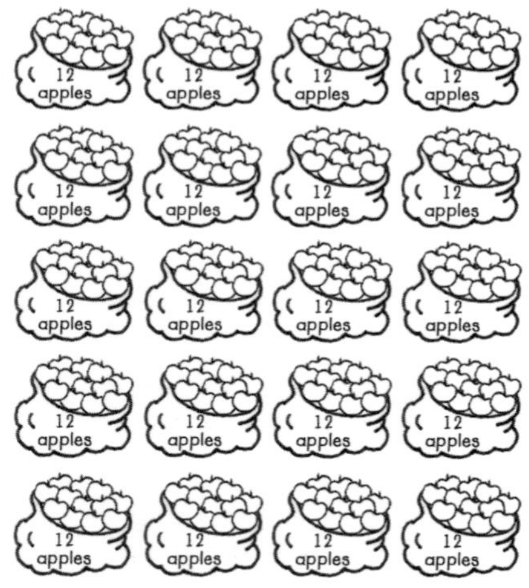

The number ____________________ is the divisor.

The number ____________________ is the quotient.

The number ____________________ is the dividend.

four	two	zero

The number ____________________ is in the ones place in the number two hundred forty.

hundreds	tens	ones
2	4	0

The number ____________________ is in the tens place in the number two hundred forty.

The number ____________________ is in the hundreds place in the number two hundred forty.

Name ______________________________

Crossword Puzzle

Look at the clues. Find the words in the word box. Write the answers in the crossword puzzle.

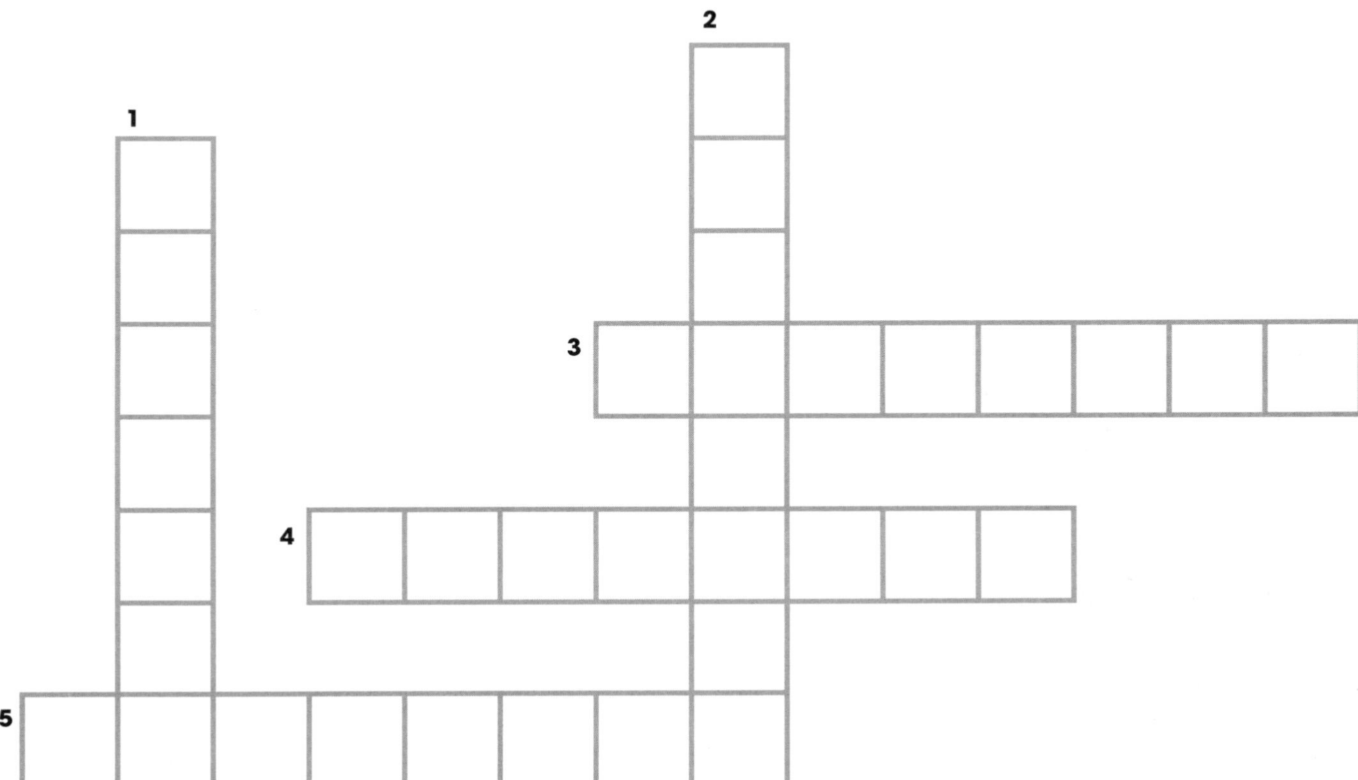

dividend

division

divisor

fraction

quotient

Clues

Down

1. the number by which a quantity is to be divided
2. inverse of multiplication

Across

3. the number to be divided
4. the answer to a division problem
5. a number that names a part of a whole or a part of a group

Name ______________________________

Assessment

Draw a circle around the answer.

In the number 4,307, which is in the hundreds place?

4	**0**	**3**

In the equation 5 ÷ 125 = 0.04, which is the divisor?

0.04	**5**	**125**

In the equation 903 ÷ 301 = 3, which is the quotient?

301	**903**	**3**

In the equation 168 ÷ 14 = 12, which is the dividend?

12	**168**	**14**

In the equation 84 ÷ 16 = 5.25, which is the decimal?

84	**16**	**5.25**

Which operation would you use to figure out a batting average?

addition	**multiplication**	**division**

In the number 42.5, which number is in the tens place?

4	**2**	**5**

Which number is a decimal?

107	**1.07**	**1,007**

Overview Geometry and Measurement

Directions and Sample Answers for Activity Pages

Day 1	See "Provide a Real-World Example" below.
Day 2	Read aloud the title and directions. Help students identify the missing word or words in each sentence and write the word or words on the line.
Day 3	Read aloud the title and directions. Help students read the clues and find answers in the word box. Model how to write a word into the crossword puzzle.
Day 4	Read aloud the title and directions. Read aloud the passage with students. Guide them to fill in the missing words using the words in the word box.
Day 5	Read aloud the directions. Allow time for students to complete the task. Afterward, meet individually with students to discuss their results. Use their responses to plan further instruction and review.

Provide a Real-World Example

- Display pictures of the Rock and Roll Hall of Fame and an Egyptian pyramid. Point to the pictures and **ask:** *What do the Rock and Roll Hall of Fame and an ancient Egyptian tomb have in common?* (Allow responses.) Then **say:** *Both structures have a pyramid shape. Ancient and modern pyramid-shaped buildings are found around the world.* Write **pyramid** and **solid shape** on chart paper or the board.

- **Say:** *A pyramid is a solid shape. What are some other three-dimensional, or solid shapes that you see every day? (cube, rectangular prism, sphere, cylinder, etc.)*

- Hand out the Day 1 activity page. Read aloud the title and directions. **Say:** *We can measure flat shapes and solid shapes in different ways. We can measure the dimensions. We can measure the length or width. We can also measure the height or depth. We can use these measurements to find the perimeter, area, surface area and volume.*

- **Say:** *A square is a flat, closed shape. We can measure the distance around the shape. We call this the perimeter. We can also measure the space that covers the shape. We call this the area. A cube is a solid shape. It's three-dimensional. We can measure the surface area of this solid. That is the total amount that covers this shape. We can also measure the volume. That is the total amount of space taken up by this shape.* Ask students to use the measurements of the shapes and the formulas to answer the questions.

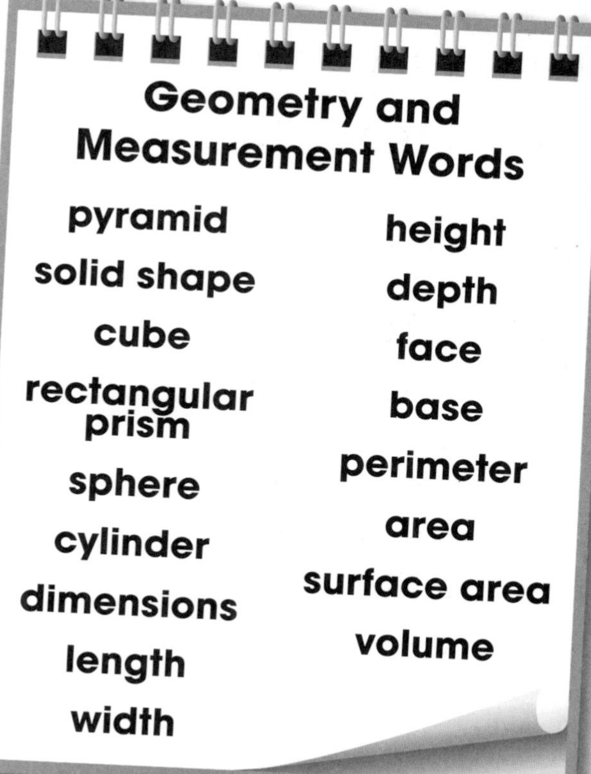

Name ______________________

Surface Area and Volume

Read each question. Write the answer on the line.

10 units

10 units

P* = 2*l* + 2*w

The perimeter of this square is

______________________ units.

A* = *l* x *w

The area of this square is

______________________ square units.

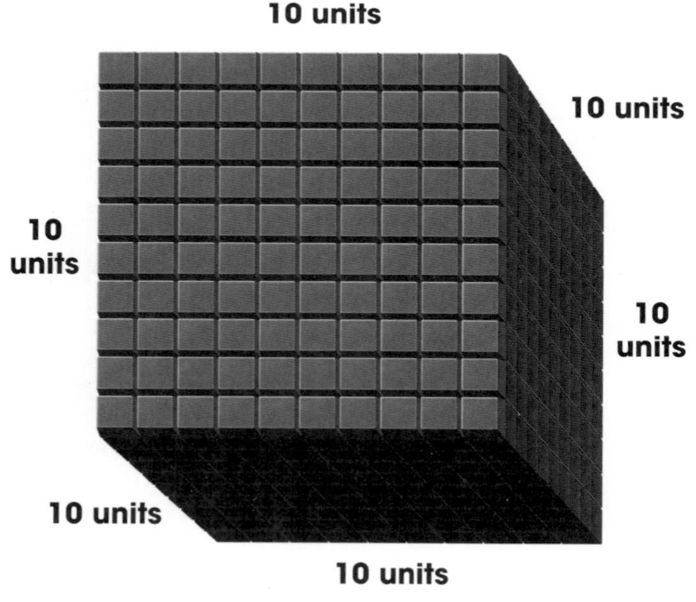

A* = *l* x *w

The area of one face of this cube is

______________________ square units.

***SA* = *l* x *w* x 6** *or* ***SA* = 6 x l^2**

The total surface area of this cube is

______________________ square units.

V* = *l* x *w* x *h *or* ***V* = l^3**

The volume of this cube is

______________________ cubic units.

Name ______________________

Cloze It Up!

Use the word or words in the word box to complete the sentences.

cube	closed shape	solid shapes	formula
length	metric units	volume	customary units

To measure ______________________, you find the distance between two points.

A square is a ______________________ because it begins and ends at the same point.

Cups, pints, quarts, and gallons are ______________________ that we can use to measure the volume of liquids.

Milliliters and liters are ______________________ that we can use to measure the volume of liquids.

Cubic inches, cubic feet, cubic centimeters, and cubic meters are all units we can use to measure the volume of ______________________.

The ______________________ for the area of a rectangle is $A = l \times w$.

The formula for the surface area of a ______________________ is $SA = 6 \times l^2$.

The ______________________ of a pyramid is equal to the *Area of the base* x *height* x *1/3*.

Name ____________________

Crossword Puzzle

Look at the clues. Find the words in the word box. Write the answers in the crossword puzzle.

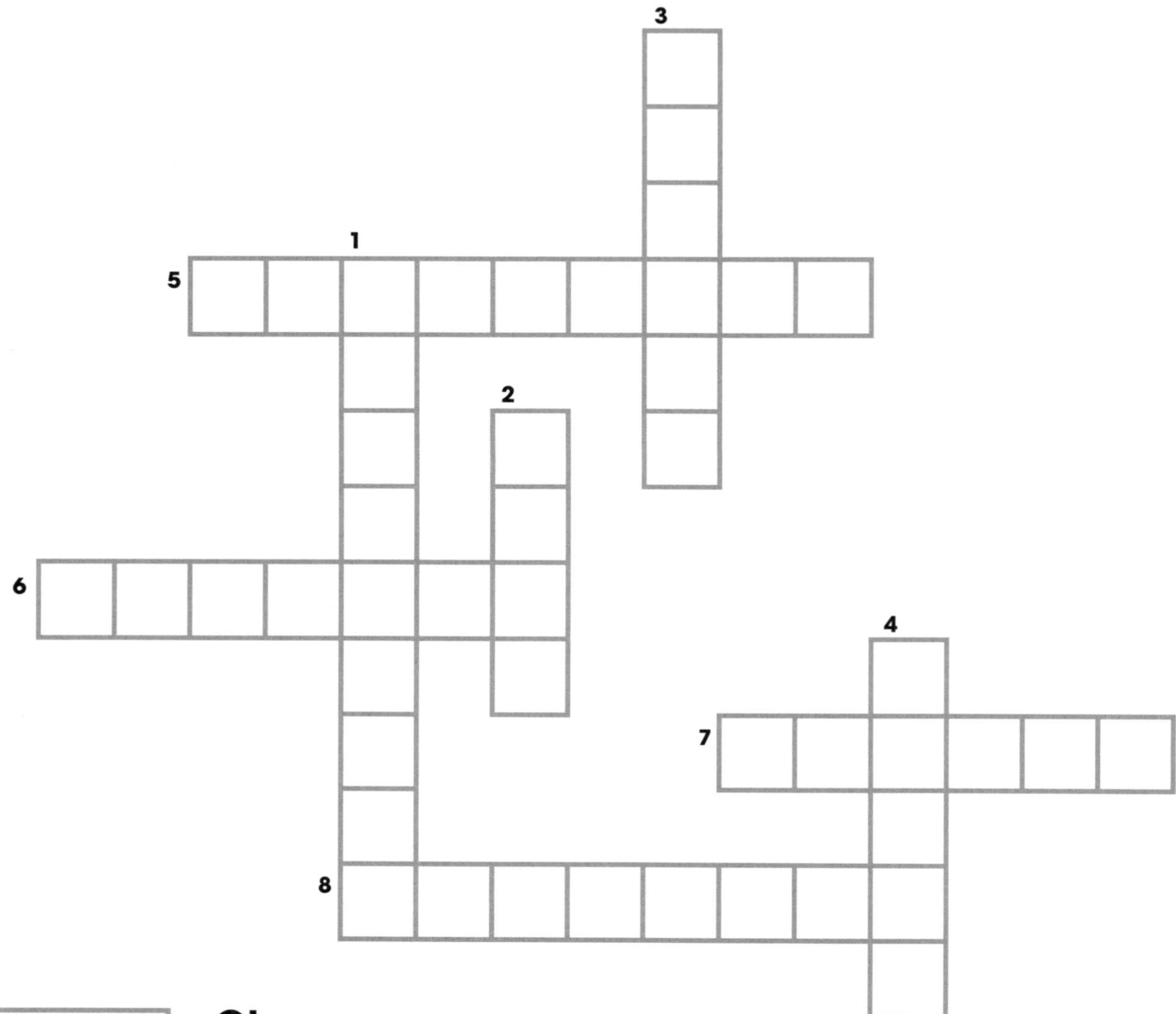

area
exponent
factor
height
perimeter
rectangle
surface
width

Clues

Down

1. a polygon with two pairs of parallel sides, two pairs of equal sides, and four right angles
2. length x width
3. you multiply it by another number to get a product
4. you multiply it by length to get the area of a rectangle

Across

5. (2 x length) + (2 x width)
6. The ______________ area is the sum of all the areas of all the faces of a solid figure.
7. measurement of how high something is
8. 8^3 ↙

 Name ______________________

List, Group, Label

Use the list of words below to complete the chart.

area	**cubic units**	**triangle**	**length**	**units**
perimeter	**pyramid**	**rectangle**	**square**	**square units**
cylinder	**rectangular prism**	**width**	**volume**	**surface area**

Shape	Measurement	Unit of Measurement

Name ____________________

Assessment

Draw a line to make a match.

distance around a shape	**exponent**
length x width x height	**height**
a rectangle has four of them	**measurements**
units for measuring volume	**perimeter**
3^2 ↙	**sides**
it's measured in square units	**surface area**
measurement from top to bottom	**volume of a rectangular prism**
length, mass, and volume	**cubic units**